Is There a Dinosaur in Your Backyard?

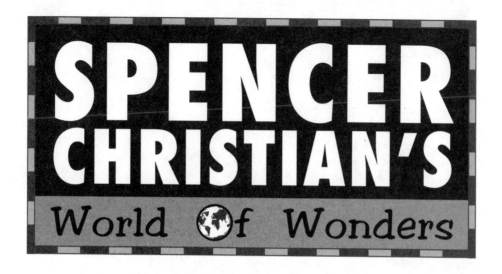

SPENCER CHRISTIAN'S
World Of Wonders

Is There a Dinosaur in Your Backyard?

THE WORLD'S MOST FASCINATING FOSSILS, ROCKS, AND MINERALS

Spencer Christian
and Antonia Felix

JOHN WILEY & SONS, INC.
New York • Chichester • Weinheim • Brisbane • Singapore • Toronto

This text is printed on acid-free paper. ∞

The publisher and the author have made every reasonable effort to ensure that the experiments and activities in this book are safe when conducted as instructed but assume no responsibility for any damage caused or sustained while performing the experiments or activities in the book. Parents, guardians, and/or teachers should supervise young readers who undertake the experiments and activities in this book.

Library of Congress Cataloging-in-Publication Data

Christian, Spencer.

    Is there a dinosaur in your backyard? : the world's most fascinating fossils, rocks, and minerals / Spencer Christian, Antonia Felix.

       p.   cm. — (Spencer Christian's world of wonders)

    Includes index.

    Summary: Text, illustrations, photographs, maps, and activities present information about rocks, minerals, fossils, and rock collecting.

    ISBN 0-471-19616-9 (paper : alk. paper)

    1. Rocks—Juvenile literature. 2. Minerals—Juvenile literature. 3. Fossils—Juvenile literature. [1. Rocks. 2. Minerals. 3. Fossils.] I. Felix, Antonia. II. Title. III. Series: Christian, Spencer. World of wonders.

    QE432.2.C48 1998

    552—dc21   97-53177

Contents

Introduction

A NATURAL HISTORY MUSEUM
RIGHT OUTSIDE YOUR DOOR

At first glance, a rock looks like a . . . lump. A slightly closer look, however, reveals that every rock has a story to tell. Some rocks have been around nearly as long as Earth itself. Some were formed out of the shells of animals that lived in the sea millions of years ago. Some formed deep in the Earth and were pushed up into the light of day in mountain ranges. Other rocks traveled through space for billions of years before running into Earth.

Rocks may be common, but there's nothing ordinary about the clues they hold to the history of Earth and to early life on this planet. In this book, we'll look at the long and sometimes bizarre road of rock history. We'll journey to Australia, where scientists found the oldest natural object on Earth. We'll explore dazzling rare stones that have been prized by kings and queens throughout the ages. We'll dig into fossils, including amazing new finds about our most ancient ancestors.

Get ready to read about these and many more amazing tales that rocks can tell!

Stone Studies

WHERE DID ALL THIS ROCK COME FROM?

Pick up a grain of sand, a pebble, or a rock, and you're holding a piece of the *crust*, or the outer layer, of Earth. **Geology,** the study of the physical history of Earth, has uncovered fascinating answers to the question of how rocks are formed. **Petrology** (from the Greek word *petros*, "stone") is the specialty in geology that deals with the study of rocks.

Modern geologists use special dating techniques to show that the first rocky crust of Earth formed from **magma** (melted rock) that cooled and hardened about 4.6 billion years ago. Earth first formed as a collection of bits of dust and gravel that collided and stuck together. These objects

came together through *gravity*, the force that attracts objects to one another. Over millions of years, more and more bits of space dust stuck together. Each collision created pressure on the growing planet, and because pressure produces heat, Earth became fiery hot.

Eventually, gases began to **rise** out of the **red-hot** mixture, forming the first **atmosphere** (the layer of oxygen and other gases that surrounds Earth). The atmosphere blocked out some of the sun's rays, allowing the surface of the hot planet to cool. Rain poured down on the hot surface, and Earth sizzled with hot steam. As it cooled, molten material hardened into blocks of Earth's first crust.

Modern geology has also discovered that rock continues to be built up and broken down in an endless cycle. New rock is constantly being created and destroyed, and various types of rocks can change from one type into another. Mountains rise up and break down. Earth's crust is on the move. Before the twentieth century, however, scientists had very different ideas about the formation of rocks—and Earth itself.

In the fifteenth and sixteenth centuries, European people thought that everything on

Old Rock Tales from around the World

People in all parts of the world have *myths* (very old stories) that explain the appearance of the first rocks on Earth:

- A myth from Polynesia tells of a magical creature named Ta'aroa, who sailed through endless space inside his shell. When he emerged, he used the shell to create rocks and soil.

- The Omaha Indians of North America believed that Earth was completely covered with water until a huge rock suddenly rose up and burst into flames. The heat dried up some of the water and uncovered the land.

- Music played a part in the creation of Earth, according to a Hopi Indian legend. The Sun God Tawa and the Earth Goddess Spider Woman together sang the First Magic Song, which made Earth form out of thin air.

- According to the Mayan culture of Latin America, Tepeu (the Creator) and Gucumatz (the Feathered Serpent) spoke the word "Earth" at the same time. In an instant, the fog began to harden into the planet Earth, the seas drew back to reveal dry land, and mountains sprang up.

- In Japanese myth, the first land on Earth was an island created by Izanagi and Izanami, brother and sister. These two creators, standing in the sky, pushed a jeweled sword down into the sea. They stirred until the water started to curdle, then pulled the sword back up. The thick goo that dripped down from the sword heaped up into an island.

- The Yauelmani Yokut Indians of California tell the story of how Eagle made the first land on Earth. Everything was covered with water, and Eagle lived in a nest in a tree branch that rose up out of the sea. He told a little duck to go to the bottom of the sea and bring back some dirt. Eagle then mixed the dirt with some crushed seeds and threw it on the water, where it swelled into a great patch of land.

Earth, from rocks and mountains to rivers and trees, was created at the same time. Using the Bible as their reference, they believed that everything in Earth's landscape formed suddenly and that any changes since then were due to great disasters such as floods and earthquakes. One scholar and cleric (church leader), Irish Archbishop James Ussher (1581–1656), claimed to have calculated the exact date of the birth of the world. Using descriptions of events from the Bible and various history books, he stated that Earth was created on Sunday, October 23rd, 4004 B.C.!

Ancient Rock Hounds

The Greek philosopher Aristotle (384–322 B.C.) and other thinkers of the ancient world had also put forth ideas about the structure of Earth. Aristotle wrote about Earth history as being a very slow process—too slow to observe in a human lifetime or even over many generations. He believed that oceans cover land and recede again in great cycles, and that the surface of Earth has always been changing, moved about by unknown forces within the planet itself.

Centuries later, the famous Persian physician, philosopher, and scientist Avicenna (A.D. 980–1037) wrote about Earth's changing face, too. According to his *Book of Minerals*, valleys were created over long periods of time, carved out by rivers. New layers of rock, called *sediments*, were formed at the bottom of the sea when small rock particles settled to the seafloor.

Taking a Closer Look

Although Aristotle and Avicenna were on the right track, their ideas were not considered by thinkers of the Middle Ages (roughly between the fifth and the fifteenth centuries). Not until the 1660s did European scientists begin to take a closer look at Earth's structure. In 1669, the Danish geologist Nicolaus Steno (1638–1686) announced two important discoveries. First, all **sedimentary rock** (rock formed by the hardening of sediment) is found in horizontal layers, one on top of the other. His second observation was that the layers at the top are youngest, and each layer below is progressively older, with the very bottom layer the oldest.

Sedimentary rock forms in horizontal layers with the oldest rock at the bottom and the youngest at the top.

Steno still held to the then-popular belief that the Earth was created in a short time, as described in the Bible. If the Earth was formed in neat, even layers, how could he explain the twisted, broken layers of rock found in mountains or other landscapes? Also, how could soft, muddy sediment be hardened into stone so quickly? Steno and others in the seventeenth century believed that such drastic changes were made by great catastrophes, as described in the Bible. The greatest of all was the Deluge, the great flood that occurred at the time of the biblical shipbuilder, Noah. Steno's theory gave credit to the Deluge for twisting up rock layers and carving deep river valleys.

Steno's principles helped miners in the 1600s and early 1700s. They could recognize rock layers and not waste time digging into an older layer that would not contain the type of rock they were looking for. Geology began to take its place as a useful science.

Digging Deeper

Philosophers and religious scholars continued to ponder the origins of Earth, a study that is called *cosmogony*. Throughout the 1700s, a volcano in Italy called Vesuvius erupted with flowing **lava** (melted rock that emerges from inside Earth and pours out of volcanoes). Scientists observed the eruptions and studied the rocks that make up the mountain. French scientist Guy Tancrède de Dolomieu (1750–1801) believed that the lava flowing out from Vesuvius came from deep inside Earth. Observing the lava eruptions, he imagined that Earth was filled with extremely hot, melted rocky material. He and other scientists figured that at one time Earth may have been a hot ball of lava-like material. When the outer layer of lava began to cool, it hardened into the rock of Earth's crust.

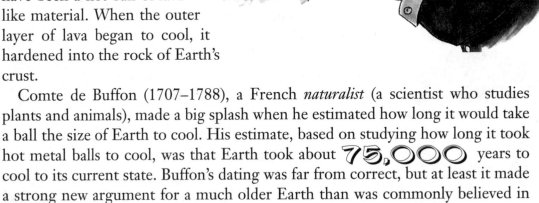

Comte de Buffon (1707–1788), a French *naturalist* (a scientist who studies plants and animals), made a big splash when he estimated how long it would take a ball the size of Earth to cool. His estimate, based on studying how long it took hot metal balls to cool, was that Earth took about **75,000** years to cool to its current state. Buffon's dating was far from correct, but at least it made a strong new argument for a much older Earth than was commonly believed in those days.

At about this time, Scottish scientist James Hutton (1726–1797) was earning his title as the father of modern geology for his groundbreaking discoveries. While observing rock formations near his home in Edinburgh, he came up with revolutionary ideas about the origins of rocks.

The landscape of Scotland's capital city proved to be a geologist's dream for Hutton. Edinburgh is built on the remains of an

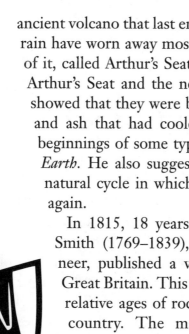

ancient volcano that last erupted 350 million years ago. Wind and rain have worn away most of the old mountain, but a big chunk of it, called Arthur's Seat, remains. Hutton studied the rock of Arthur's Seat and the nearby hills called Salisbury Crags. He showed that they were built up from **many** layers of lava and ash that had cooled. Hutton wrote about the volcanic beginnings of some types of rock in his book *A Theory of the Earth*. He also suggested, for the first time, that there is a natural cycle in which rock forms, is broken up, and forms again.

In 1815, 18 years after Hutton's death, William Smith (1769–1839), a clever English engineer, published a very special map of Great Britain. This map showed the relative ages of rock layers in that country. The map backed up Hutton's claim that Earth must be millions of years old and constantly changing. How did Smith uncover different ages for rock—something that no one had done before? Fossils!

A **fossil,** which we'll explore in detail in Chapter 5, is the remains of, or the impression left by, a plant or animal. William Smith was hired to build a canal in England. Digging through the earth, he took a close look at the fossils that appeared in each layer of rock. There was a pattern—each layer of rock held its own type of fossil. If the same fossil was found in two different types

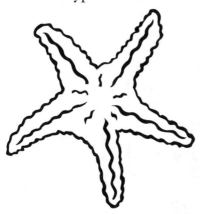

of rock, Smith figured that the rocks had to be the same age. He further theorized that rocks found in different parts of the country would also be the same age if they contained the same fossils. Smith traveled all over England, Wales, and Scotland, comparing rocks and the fossils contained in them. He put that information on his map.

Another Scottish geologist, Sir Charles Lyell (1797–1875), presented a theory that explains the gradual change of Earth's structure over time. His theory of *uniformitarianism* (the **longest** word in this book, I promise!) states that rock is formed in a slow, "uniform" way,

through a variety of processes. Lyell's Earth-shaping forces include volcanic eruptions, uplifting movements from deep within Earth, and wind and rain, which break down rock.

Earth's Deep Secret

The next big step in geology came quite recently. In the 1950s, when I was in grade school and just starting to get interested in rocks, scientists unlocked a deep secret of Earth. At the bottom of the oceans lies a long string of mountains called the **midocean ridges.** Scientists had detected underwater mountains with the invention of sonar during World War I. *Sonar* uses sound waves to measure the distance between a ship and objects on the ocean floor. In the 1950s, the U.S. Navy used high-tech sonar to carefully measure and map these mountain ranges for the first time. They discovered many more mountains than anyone had imagined. The midocean ridges stretch 40,000 miles (64,400 km) around the entire planet. On a computer-made map, Earth's underwater mountains look like the stitches that cover a baseball.

By comparing maps that were made at different times, scientists saw that the ocean crust is moving. The tops of the midocean ridges have a wide *trough,* or valley, instead of pointed tips like land mountains. Lava flows from the troughs through *fissures* (cracks) and hardens into rock. When new lava flows through the cracks, it slowly pushes the old crust away on both sides of the mountain ridge. This movement is called **seafloor spreading** and occurs at the rate of about

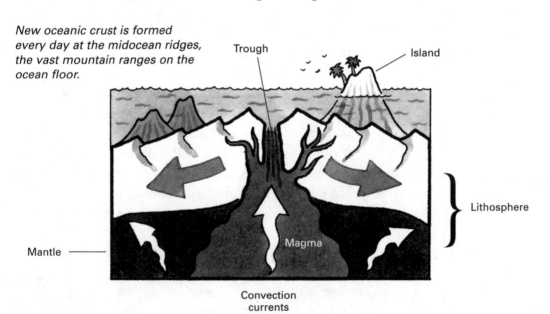

New oceanic crust is formed every day at the midocean ridges, the vast mountain ranges on the ocean floor.

Trough

Island

Lithosphere

Mantle

Magma

Convection currents

Pangaea

Plate tectonics explained a mystery that had baffled scientists for hundreds of years. Why do the continents look as though they could fit together like pieces in a puzzle? Did they break apart from one huge continent? In the early 1900s, German scientist Alfred Wegener (1880–1930) suggested that in the distant past, the continents were all joined as one giant supercontinent he called Pangaea (pronounced pan-*jee*-ya). He believed that this continent slowly broke apart and the pieces drifted away from each other. His theory explained why the continents look like puzzle pieces and why fossils of the exact same plants and animals were found on different continents. At the time, Wegener's ideas were considered too fantastic to be true. Many years later, however, the theory of plate tectonics revealed that Wegener was right.

half an inch (1–2 cm) per day. Thanks to sonar, scientists discovered that new oceanic crust is constantly being formed at the midocean ridges.

The nonstop flow of magma up toward these fissures is caused by **convection currents.** Heat makes air or liquid (even thick, heavy liquid such as magma) move. Hot air or liquid moves up into cooler areas, and convection currents below the midocean ridges move magma toward the surface in regular pathways.

The discovery of the midocean ridges helped geologists make a new map of Earth's crust. They discovered that the crust is split up into several pieces. These pieces, called **tectonic plates,** move around on the **mantle,** the liquid rock layer that lies below Earth's crust. The discovery of these movements, called *plate tectonics*, reveals that the face of Earth is changing all the time.

Even though new oceanic crust is being formed every day, it isn't just piling up. Nature's recycling program pushes old oceanic crust back down into the magma at the edge of the plate opposite a midocean ridge. The edge of one oceanic plate slides beneath another plate and is pushed down into the hot mantle. There it melts into magma, returning to its original form.

The next time you visit the ocean or see a picture of it, think about the amazing rock-recycling program that is slowly churning away on the ocean floor. You can read all about the tectonic plates and underwater volcanoes in my book *Shake, Rattle, and Roll*.

The Invisible World

Technology has given scientists an idea of what makes up the inside of Earth. If the deepest drill can only reach 9 miles (15 km) beneath the surface, that leaves about 3,950 miles (6,360 km) to go to get to the center of Earth! How do scientists learn about underground places that they cannot see? To study Earth's deep layers, scientists use a *seismograph*, an instrument that records *seismic* (shock) *waves* (the energy released from an earthquake). Seismic waves bend or bounce off different types of material beneath Earth's surface and help scientists understand what kind of material lies deep within the Earth. This information is used to create a model of Earth made of three main layers: the outer crust, the mantle (containing magma), and the core.

Two types of crust make up the thin outer layer of Earth: (1) *Oceanic crust*, beneath the oceans, is made primarily of a rock called basalt; and (2) continental crust, which holds the land we live on, is made primarily of granite rock. Crust takes up 0.8 percent of Earth's total volume.

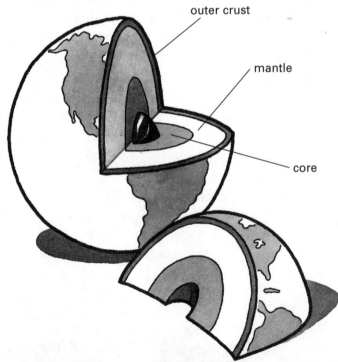

Earth is made of three main layers: the outer crust, the mantle, and the core.

outer crust

mantle

core

EXPERIMENT

WAVES THAT BOUNCE

In this experiment, you'll use sound waves to explore how seismic waves react when they hit different substances in Earth's interior.

What You Need:

- An experiment partner

- Several books—enough to make two equal stacks about 3 inches (7.6 cm) high

- Two cardboard toilet-paper tubes, or 1 paper-towel tube cut into two equal halves

- Ticking watch

- Glass plate

- Cork coaster

What to Do:

1. Place the two stacks of books on a desk or table.
2. Place one tube diagonally on each stack, to make an upside-down **V** shape (see the illustration).
3. Ask your partner to place the watch at the opening of one of the tubes, at the wide end of the **V**.
4. Put your ear up to the opening of the other tube, also at the wide end of the **V**, and listen.
5. Ask your partner to place a plate at the opposite end of the tubes, where they come together to form the narrow tip of the **V**.
6. Listen again.
7. Ask your friend to replace the plate with the cork coaster.
8. Listen a third time.

continued

continued

What Happens and Why:

With no plate, you cannot hear the watch tick through the other tube. When the glass plate is put at the other end, however, the sound waves of the ticking watch bounce off the plate and travel down the other tube. As a result, you can hear the sound waves. When the cork coaster is used, however, the cork absorbs the sound waves, so the waves do not bounce back to you, and you cannot hear them.

This is similar to what happens when seismic waves travel through rock inside Earth. Some waves pass through material, like the sound waves that go through the tube and into the air; other waves hit solid material and bounce to the surface of Earth, like the sound waves that bounce off the plate; and some waves are slowed down or absorbed, like the sound waves that are soaked up by the cork.

Beneath the crust lies the mantle, made of extremely hot, melted rock material called magma. This is the largest portion of Earth, taking up 83 percent of the volume of the planet.

The central core of Earth is a solid globe made of iron, a very heavy *element* (type of chemical). Iron sank to the deepest section of Earth while the planet was being formed. The **weight** of the mantle and crust bearing down from all sides puts an enormous amount of pressure on the core. This **pressure** pushes the iron into a solid ball that takes up about 16.2 percent of Earth's volume.

Going to the Core: Geology's Hottest New Discovery

As this century is closing and a new one begins, geologists have made a surprising new discovery about Earth's core. In 1996, scientists from Columbia University in New York announced that the solid inner core of Earth is spinning

Geologic Time Warp:
The Age of the Earth Scaled to One Year

Date	Time	Event
January 1	Midnight	Earth formed (fiery ball of magma)
March 15		First rock formed (that has been dated)
April 1		Life begins as one-celled creatures in the oceans
November 15		First land plants and animals
December 15 to December 26		Age of dinosaurs
December 31	Near midnight: 11:58:45	Last Ice Age
	11:59:45 to 11:59:50	Rise and Fall of the Roman Empire
	11:59:57	Columbus reaches America
	11:59:59	Geology has been a science for only one second!

freely and slightly faster than the rest of the planet. Just a bit smaller than the moon, the inner core is like a planet within a planet! The structure of Earth is more complex and mysterious than scientists ever imagined.

New, high-tech methods of measuring seismic waves brought about this breakthrough, which ushers in a new chapter in geology. It ignites new studies about how Earth's interior developed over the ages and how heat flows through Earth. What other secrets are hidden in Earth's unseen interior—and who will uncover them?

Rocks
A WORLD OF INCREDIBLE VARIETY

A tiny grain of sand at the beach, a beautifully cut diamond the size of your fist, a glimmering black boulder along the highway, a slab of crust stretching beneath the Pacific Ocean for thousands of miles—rocks come in an **amazing** variety of shapes and sizes.

A **rock** is a natural solid object made of one or more minerals. A **mineral** is a nonliving (inorganic), solid, natural substance. (We'll dig into minerals in Chapter 3.) Minerals come in many varieties, and the mineral particles that make up rocks are called **grains.** Some rocks have grains that are large enough to be seen by the unaided eye, and others contain very tiny grains that can only be seen with a microscope. The size of a rock's grains make up the rock's *texture*. About 100 rocks are listed in any basic field guide, but all rocks fall into one of three main families: igneous, sedimentary, or metamorphic. The three basic types of rock are defined by the way in which they are formed.

Igneous Rock

Igneous rock is formed from molten rock inside Earth that cools and hardens. There are two types of igneous rock—one that forms below the surface and one that forms aboveground.

Intrusive igneous rock is the first type, formed when molten rock squeezes up into a cooler level of the crust and hardens. Intrusive rocks only appear on the surface after the rock above them has worn away, or when forces beneath push them up. **Extrusive igneous rock** is formed when lava erupts from volcanoes and cracks in the earth. Once it reaches the surface, the melted rock cools and hardens.

Most of Earth's crust, about 90 percent, is made of igneous rock. All of the original rock on Earth was igneous, formed when Earth's outermost layer of fiery magma hardened for the first time.

Intrusive igneous rocks include granite, diorite, and gabbro. Granite is the most common rock found on Earth's surface. It forms below the surface, but erosion and uplift has exposed granite throughout the world. Because intrusive rocks form underground, they cool and harden more slowly than extrusive rocks,

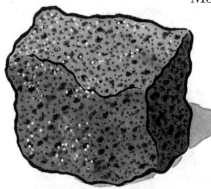

Granite, an intrusive igneous rock, is speckled with large grains.

Mighty Magma

Magma, which forms igneous rock when it cools and hardens, is hot stuff below the surface, ranging from 950° to 7,500° Fahrenheit (500° to 4,150° Celsius). How far below the surface of Earth does magma lie? You'd have to drill about 40 miles (60 km) to reach the first layer of magma. No one has ever drilled deeper than about 9 miles (15 km) down. Scientists learn about magma by observing lava flows, studying igneous rocks, and—as discussed in Chapter 1—reading the paths of seismic waves.

which cool outside. That **difference** in cooling speed gives intrusive rocks a course-grained texture and extrusive rocks a fine-grained texture. The speckled, salt-and-pepper look of intrusive rocks such as granite and diorite contrasts with the smooth, glassy look of extrusive rocks such as obsidian and felsite.

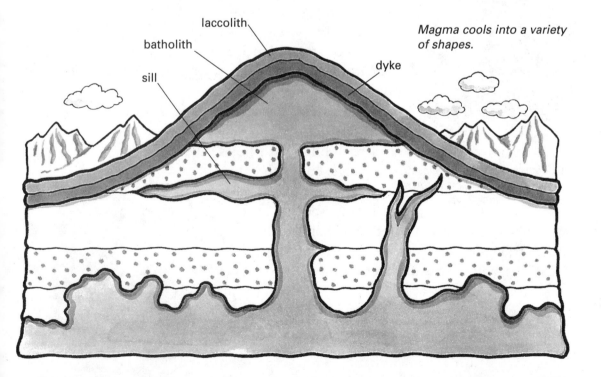

Magma cools into a variety of shapes.

World-Record Rock

In 1996, scientists announced the discovery of the world's deepest rock. The garnet peridotite, an intrusive igneous rock, was found in the Swiss Alps. The scientists determined that the rock originally formed more than 186 miles (300 km) deep in Earth's crust. The ongoing upward thrust of the Alps gradually pushed the rock to the surface. This is the deepest rock ever brought to the surface by natural forces.

ntrusive igneous rocks create a variety of formations within the crust. A **dyke** is formed by magma that rises up through layers of rock in a wall-like structure. A **sill** spreads out between rock layers to create a horizontal sheet of igneous rock. A **laccolith** forms the shape of a dome that pushes up the crust above. The largest formation is a **batholith,** an enormous pool of magma that takes thousands of years to cool.

Common extrusive igneous rocks are basalt, rhyolite, and andesite. Basalt is the black rock that forms after a lava flow. The new ocean crust that forms out of lava flows at the ocean ridges is also basalt. The islands of Hawaii are great mountains of basalt, formed by repeated eruptions of lava.

Some extrusive rocks, such as pumice and scoria, are formed from explosive lava eruptions. Violent volcanic explosions shoot out lava that is filled with gas. Frothy pieces of this gas-filled lava cool very quickly into pumice. *Pumice* is a rock filled with holes, like a sponge, and is so light that it floats on water. *Scoria* is also spongy look-

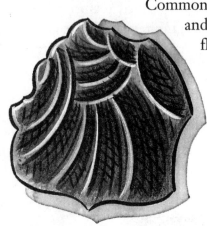

Obsidian, a smooth and glassy extrusive igneous rock, is formed by rapidly cooling lava.

ing but is darker and heavier than pumice. It is formed from lava that does not have as much gas mixed in it, and it sinks in water.

Explosive eruptions of lava form pumice, a very light rock that floats on water.

EXPERIMENT

LAVA PUFFS!

Rock such as basalt forms when lava seeps out over the surface during volcanic activity. Here's a very tasty way to look at how lava breaks through Earth's crust and hardens on the surface. In this case, we'll use strawberry jam to represent red-hot lava in a batch of tarts I call Lava Puffs! **This activity requires adult supervision.**

What You Need:
- Muffin tin

- Cooking-oil spray

- Pastry crust (The easiest kind to use is premade pie crust, folded and ready to use, from the grocery store's refrigerator section. You can also use the frozen pie crust that comes in a tin pie pan—thaw the crust first, and remove it from the pan.)

- Round pastry cutter or drinking glass

- Spoon

- Strawberry jam

- Toothpick

- Oven mitts

What to Do:
1. Ask an adult to preheat the oven to 400° F. (204° C).
2. Spray the inside of each cup in the muffin tin with cooking oil.
3. Spread the piece of pastry crust out flat, and cut out circles

continued

EXPERIMENT

continued

with the pastry cutter. If you don't have a pastry cutter, use a drinking glass, pressing the open side of the glass into the pastry to cut it.

4. Place a circle of pastry on the bottom of each muffin cup.
5. Drop one spoonful of strawberry jam onto the pastry round in each muffin cup.
6. Place another pastry round on top of the jam in each muffin cup.
7. Press along the sides to seal the top pastry round with the bottom pastry round.
8. Using the toothpick, make a small hole in the top of each pastry circle.
9. Bake the tarts for about 15–20 minutes. Ask your adult helper to check them while they bake, and to take them out when they're golden brown using oven mitts.
10. Allow the tarts to cool slightly before taking them out of the muffin tin.
11. Taste!

What Happens and Why:
When the air heats up inside the tart, the heat forces the jam to move. The jam escapes through the hole in the top crust, just like magma escapes through a weak point or crack in Earth's crust. After the tart cools, the jam on top hardens slightly. This represents lava that hardens into rock as it cools.

Igneous Rock Is Like Ice Cream!

Igneous rock and ice cream both start out as liquids and cool down to become solid, and both will melt again if the temperature gets hot enough!

Sedimentary Rock

Sedimentary rock is formed from pieces of surface rock that sink to the bottoms of large bodies of water such

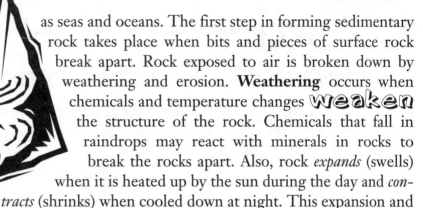

as seas and oceans. The first step in forming sedimentary rock takes place when bits and pieces of surface rock break apart. Rock exposed to air is broken down by weathering and erosion. **Weathering** occurs when chemicals and temperature changes **weaken** the structure of the rock. Chemicals that fall in raindrops may react with minerals in rocks to break the rocks apart. Also, rock *expands* (swells) when it is heated up by the sun during the day and *contracts* (shrinks) when cooled down at night. This expansion and contraction causes **cracks** to form in the rock. Weather events can affect rock in another way, too: When water seeps into cracks and freezes, the resulting ice expands and cracks the rock further.

Wind that carries sand and other tiny particles attacks rock through **erosion,** wearing it away at the surface. Eroded pieces of rock fall to the ground and get washed by rain into streams or rivers. Some of the particles of rock, called **sediment,** are carried by the rivers to the sea. Sediment can also include broken seashells and the remains of small sea animals.

The sediment settles to the seafloor, where new layers of sediment will gradually build up over it. The pressure of millions of tons of piled-up sediment helps transform the layers into solid rock. Sedimentary rock always forms in *strata* (layers).

Though most sediment deposits occur on the ocean floor, some are also found on land and in lakes. Geologists group sedimentary rocks into three groups, according to the type of material that forms them: clastic sediments, chemical sediments, and organic sediments. **Clastic sediments** are made of rocks ranging in size from fine particles of clay to boulders. Carried by the wind or in streams to a large body of water, the rock sinks to the bottom. The pressure of layer upon layer **squeezes** water out of the sediment, and chemicals work as natural cement to bind the rock particles together. These chemicals may be left behind from the water or they may be in the mineral sediments. This process turns silt, a rock particle smaller than a sand grain but larger than a clay grain, into *siltstone*. Clay sediments turn into a rock called *shale*.

THE LAYERED LOOK—MAKING SEDIMENTARY ROCKS

Through the process of **lithification** (stone forming), particles of sediment turn into solid rock. This takes millions of years in nature, but you can make sedimentary rock in your kitchen in four days!

What You Need:

• 33.8 oz. (1 liter) plastic soda bottle (with labels removed)

• 2 glass mixing bowls

• 4 cups (1 liter) sand

• 2 cups (0.5 liter) plaster of Paris

• Water

• Food coloring, four colors

• Scissors

What to Do:

1. Cut off the top, curved part of the plastic bottle.
2. Mix two cups of sand and one cup of plaster of Paris together in a glass mixing bowl.
3. Sprinkle in water to dampen the mixture, and stir. Add just enough water to make the mixture moist, but not runny.
4. Place half of this mixture into the other bowl.
5. Stir a few drops of food coloring into each bowl. Use different colors for each bowl.
6. Press the contents of one bowl into the bottom of the plastic soda bottle. On top of that, press the contents of the second bowl.
7. Rinse out the mixing bowls.
8. Repeat steps 2 through 6, using two more food colors.
9. Set the bottle aside to harden for four days.
10. Remove the rock by carefully cutting the bottle with the scissors.

continued

continued

What Happens and Why:
Just like the chemicals that bind rock particles together into sedimentary rocks, the plaster of Paris cements the sand grains together. Each colored layer represents a stratum of rock. In nature, pressure also acts on the sediment to bind it together into rock over time. In this experiment, the strong binding action of the plaster represents the power of pressure to form rock.

Sand is bound together to form *sandstone*. Smooth pebbles can be pressed together to form *conglomerate rock*, also called *pudding stone*. Chunky, sharp-edged rocks cement together to form *breccias*.

One of the most awesome examples of clastic sedimentary rock is found in the Grand Canyon in the western United States. Layer upon layer of shale, sandstone, and limestone, formed beneath ancient seas, are exposed in a majestic geology exhibit—thanks to the Colorado River. For about 6 million years, the mighty Colorado has **crashed** over the rock, cutting through it to form wide-open canyons. The oldest rock layer, at the bottom of the canyon, is about 2 billion years old.

Smooth pebbles cemented together with chemicals and minerals form pudding stone.

The second type of sedimentary rock is **chemical sediment.** Minerals floating in water are exposed to the air when the water *evaporates* (turns from a liquid into vapor). Released from the water, the minerals solidify into hard substances. In this way, silica forms beds of *flint* rock, sodium chloride becomes *rock salt*, and iron oxide becomes *iron ore*. One of nature's most ⓐⓌⒺⓈⓄⓂⒺ designs is the transformation of calcite into *limestone*. Underground caves can contain a dazzling variety of limestone formations, including *stalactites*, objects shaped like icicles that hang from the cave ceiling. These amazing cave structures are discussed in detail in my book *What Makes the Grand Canyon Grand?*

The third type of sedimentary rock, **organic sediment,** is made from the remains of living things such as plants and shellfish. Shells and tiny skeletons of water creatures sink to the ocean floor to form layers that, in time, bind together

Limestone is a type of chemical sedimentary rock that forms into stalactites, stalagmites, and many other objects in caves.

into rock. The rock that makes up the famous white cliffs of Dover, on the southeast coast of England, is *chalky limestone*, formed from the shells of one-celled organisms called *foraminifera*. Coral is the rocklike outer skeleton of an underwater creature called the *coral polyp*. Grouped together into underwater beds called *coral reefs*, coral and crushed shells harden into rock called *fossiliferous limestone*.

Coal is an organic sedimentary rock formed from the remains of plants that sank into swamps millions of years ago. Coal can be burned to produce **heat** or to **power** an engine. The first step in making coal began in thick, swampy forests that covered parts of North America, Asia, and Europe from

Pipestone: Blood of the People

More than 400 years ago, Native Americans of the Great Plains began to *quarry* (remove from the ground) a red stone in what is now southwestern Minnesota. According to legend, the creator Tonkashula told the people that the red stone was very precious, as it contained the blood of their ancestors. This stone, which is called *pipestone* or *catlinite*, was formed when ancient beds of clay solidified into sedimentary rock.

People from many tribes, including the Crow, Blackfoot, Pawnee, and Sioux, traveled for thousands of miles to quarry the soft, red, easy-to-carve stone. The quarry was considered sacred land, and special ceremonies were performed throughout the process of taking the stone from the quarry. One of the stone's main uses was to carve the bowl of the peace pipe, which was used in many ceremonies (the stem of the pipe was made from wood). Although the land on

which the pipestone quarry lies no longer belongs to Native Americans, it has been protected as a national monument, and only Native Americans are allowed to quarry the pipestone. Keeping with the quarry's long and peaceful tradition, drills and explosives are not allowed—only hand tools, such as sledgehammers, chisels, and shovels, can be used.

Hard-Hitting Tools

Like all other sedimentary rock, flint forms in layers. This makes flint easy to split and shape into sharp edges. Early humans fashioned flint into handmade tools, such as axes, daggers, sickles, spearheads, and arrowheads. A Stone Age (300,000 to 1 million years ago) hand ax was a piece of flint with sharp edges, used to cut wood and plants, to skin animals, and to chop up animal bones.

hand ax   cleaver   double-edge scraper

chopping tool   borer   spearhead

Humans' first tools were hand-held, sharpened pieces of flint called hand axes.

about 270 to 350 million years ago. Thick beds of rotting vegetation piled up in the swamps. Squeezed and compacted, the vegetation turned into *peat,* which is about 90 percent water. In time, the peat compressed into a brown, crumbly substance called *lignite,* which contains about 50 percent water. Time and pressure worked on the lignite to squeeze it into a harder substance, *bituminous coal,* also known as household coal. This brittle coal is covered in black powder that comes off in your hands and makes coal mining a **very dirty** business! The oldest coal, *anthracite,* is harder than household coal and does not have a powdery finish. Clean and shiny, anthracite is the highest-quality coal because it gives off the most energy and burns without much smoke.

Metamorphic Rock

Metamorphic rock starts out as igneous or sedimentary rock and is changed by heat and pressure deep inside Earth. Most metamorphic rock is formed where a new mountain range is being thrust up. Mountain building, which is explored in my book *Shake, Rattle, and Roll*, takes place when tectonic plates *collide*. Rock at the edges of the plates is thrust deep into the earth, where enormous heat and pressure act on it. As the big squeeze continues, the rock is forced up, twist-

Doorkeepers in the Dark

During the Industrial Revolution in England in the 1800s, many boys and girls were sent to work in the underground coal mines. I once visited a mining museum and mine in Wales and learned a lot about the horrible conditions some of the miners endured.

I will never forget the story of the children, some as young as age six, who were employed as doorkeepers, miles below the surface in the depths of the mines. A *doorkeeper* would sit by a door and listen for footsteps or the creak of a coal cart, then open the door and allow the miner or cart to pass through to another section of the mine. What's so awful about that? It sounds like easy work, but the child would sit in *pitch dark* and *total silence* for up to 12 hours a day! The lucky doorkeepers were those who shared a tiny passageway, one at

each door—at least they had someone to talk to through the long, dark hours.

Children also worked as cart pushers in the mines. In 1842, nine-year-old Edward Edwards described his job: "I drag carts loaded with coal from the coalface to the main road, a distance of sixty yards. There are no wheels to the carts . . . sometimes the cart is pushed on to us and we get crushed often."

Oldest Rock Is a New Find

The oldest rocks discovered so far on Earth's crust were found in Canada. The *acasta gneisses* are a block of metamorphic rocks dated to be 4 billion years old. They lie about 200 miles north of Yellowknife, Northwest Territories, and were discovered in the late 1980s.

ing and folding into a mountain range. The heat and pressure are so great that they change the *crystal structure*—the way the molecules fit together—of the igneous or sedimentary rock, turning it into a new kind of rock altogether. (We explore a rock's crystal structure in Chapter 3.) *Metamorphic* comes from the Greek words *meta*, ("change") and *morphic*, ("shape").

Rocks That Grew on Trees!

Arizona's Petrified Forest National Park is filled with the remains of trees that flourished in North America's forests about 225 million years ago. Like mummies, they have been preserved forever—but these mummies turned to stone!

When the trees died, they fell into swampy water containing minerals and chemicals. Some of the minerals in the water came from ash that had spewed out of volcanoes. The minerals seeped into the buried logs as they began to decay in the soupy swamp. Over time, the minerals filled up the spaces within the tree's cells and hardened into rock, keeping the perfect form of the tree trunk. Wood that has been preserved in this way is called **petrified wood**. Petrifying adds a new rainbow of color to the once-brown wood. Iron oxide stains the wood orange, rust, red, or yellow. Manganese oxide produces blues, blacks, or purples. One of nature's most distinctive rocks, petrified wood is found in many places once covered by prehistoric forests, from North and South America to Europe and the Middle East.

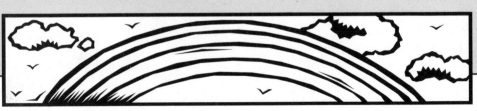

Magma beneath the surface creates an aureole, a halo of heat in the surrounding rock that transforms it into metamorphic rock.

In addition to forming during mountain building, metamorphic rock can also be formed around intrusions of magma such as batholiths and dykes. Molten rock that pushes up into the crust **heats** the surrounding rock. This halo of metamorphic rock is called an **aureole.**

Marble is a metamorphic rock made from limestone. Formed in a variety of spectacular patterns, marble has been the building and sculpting stone of choice, starting with the ancient Greeks and Romans. Granite transforms into the metamorphic rock gneiss, and sandstone changes into quartzite. Slate is a metamorphic rock formed from shale and clay.

Marble That Made History

Italy's Carrara quarry is home of the world's most famous marble, used to create legendary works of art. The Italian painter and sculptor Michelangelo (1475–1564) used marble from this quarry to sculpt statues, such as *David*, which are some of the greatest artworks of all time.

A Table of Common Rocks

Igneous Rocks

Rock	Color	Structure
Granite	White to gray, pink to red	Medium-to-coarse, tightly arranged crystals
Gabbro	Greenish-gray to black	Coarse crystals
Peridotite	Greenish-gray	Coarse crystals
Basalt	Dark greenish-gray to black	Microscopic crystals
Pumice	Grayish-white	Light, fine pores; floats on water
Obsidian	Black, sometimes with brown streaks	Glassy

Sedimentary Rocks

Rock	Color	Structure
Breccia	Gray to black, tan to red	Sharp pieces of rock bound together by natural cement
Shale	Yellow, red, gray, green, black	Soft, fine particles; splits easily
Sandstone	White, gray, yellow, red	Fine or coarse grains, naturally cemented together
Limestone	White, gray, and buff to black and red	Very fine grains, forms in thick beds
Flint	Dark gray, brown, black	Hard and glassy
Coal	Dull black to shiny black	Brittle

Metamorphic Rocks

Rock	Color	Structure
Marble	Many colors, often mixed	Medium to coarse crystals
Slate	Black, red, green, purple	Fine grains, splits easily into thin slabs
Gneiss	Gray and pink to black and red	Stripes of medium to coarse crystals
Quartzite	White, gray, pink, buff	Hard and glassy
Schist	White, gray, red, green, black	Flaky particles; sparkles, feels slippery
Amphibolite	Light green to black	Hard, fine-to-coarse grains; sparkles

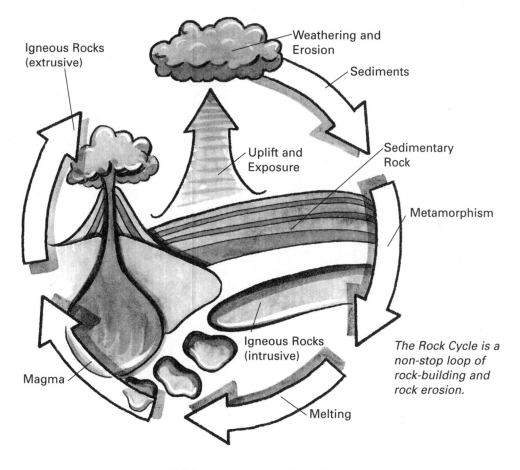

Igneous Rocks (extrusive)

Weathering and Erosion

Sediments

Uplift and Exposure

Sedimentary Rock

Metamorphism

Magma

Igneous Rocks (intrusive)

Melting

The Rock Cycle is a non-stop loop of rock-building and rock erosion.

The Rock Cycle

The surface of Earth is continually renewed through the **rock cycle.** Rock is worn away by wind and rain and is washed away to sea. Settling to the bottom, it hardens into sediment. Heat and pressure turn deeply buried sedimentary rock into metamorphic rock. Metamorphic rock may be lifted up to the surface. If heated enough, metamorphic rock may also melt to become new magma. Magma cools into igneous rock or flows to the surface as lava. As soon as it is exposed to the elements of wind and rain, rock begins to wear away, and the cycle begins again.

Rocks of Wonder:
Spencer's Handpicked List of Amazing Rocks

Name	Location	Description
Devil's Tower	Wyoming, U.S.	The plug, or central core, of an ancient volcano. The lava cooled and hardened into igneous rock and is all that remains after the softer outer layer of the volcanic mountain eroded away.

Name	Location	Description
Le Puy	France	Another volcano plug—with a church built on top!

Name	Location	Description
Giant's Causeway Basalt Columns	Northern Ireland	A massive field of *hexagonal* (six-sided) columns of basalt rock. It looks like sculpture!

continued

Rocks of Wonder • continued

Name	Location	Description
Pele's Hair	Hawaii	Tiny jets of lava spray quickly cooled into light-brown fibers of basalt that look exactly like hair! Named after Pele, the Hawaiian fire goddess.

Name	Location	Description
Balanced Rock	Colorado, U.S.	Perched delicately on a tiny base of rock, this huge block of sandstone looks as if it could fall over with one flick of your finger! Once surrounded by softer rock, erosion gradually exposed this amazing round sandstone formation.

Name	Location	Description
Itacolumite— "bendable rock"	North Carolina, U.S. and India	This very rare sandstone forms in thin strips that can be bent by hand!

Slow Soil

It takes about 100 years for 1 inch (2.5 cm) of soil to form on the forest floor.

Rock Garden

Soil, one of Earth's most precious natural resources, couldn't exist without rock. *Soil* is a mixture of minerals, organic (living) particles, air, and water. Most life on Earth depends on soil for food, as it contains **nutrients** (nourishing substances) that are essential to plants and the animals that eat them.

Soil forms slowly, and it all begins with the weathering of rock. Rain, ice, and the processes of freezing and thawing crack and crumble Earth's crust. Tiny, simple plants called *lichens* live on the decaying rock, and when they die, their organic matter mixes with the crumbling rock. Other plants and animals also die, leaving their

Earthworms—Nature's Recycler

Earthworms are very important residents of soil because they recycle decayed material in the soil into food that nurtures plants. Earthworms eat just about anything they find—leaves, fruit, stones, bones, and other bits of dead insects and animals—and pass it out of their bodies back into the soil. The food a worm eats undergoes chemical changes in its digestive system and is deposited back into the soil as new, improved material called a *worm cast*.

In India in the 1980s, farmers began using worm cast as fertilizer for crops. They discovered that worm cast created such rich soil that there was almost no more need for chemical fertilizer. News of earthworm fertilizer, called *vermicompost*, spread throughout the world, and earthworms are becoming the stars of organic farming! Not only do the worms enrich soil with their worm cast, but they also eat waste products from paper mills and food-processing plants, which would otherwise pollute the land.

Monster worm: The longest earthworm in the world, found in South Africa in 1937, measured 22 feet (6.7 m) long!

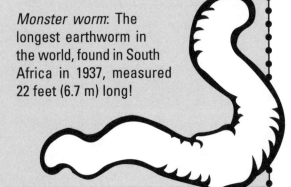

remains on the rocky soil. Tiny plants and animals called fungi and microbes break down the decaying remains and other organic matter into basic nutrients.

Organic material, combined with water and minerals in the rock, supports the growth of more tiny plants and of animals that eat those plants. Animals such as ants, termites, snails, and earthworms help mix up the minerals and *humus* (a jellylike mix of dead leaves, insects, and other animals) as they move around in the soil. The tunnels of worms keep the soil soft and loose so that rain can soak down to the roots of plants. In this way, the parent rock is broken down into fine particles of sand, silt, and clay.

3

Minerals

WORTH THEIR WEIGHT IN GOLD (OR SILVER, OR MICA, OR . . .)

On a visit to the Smithsonian Museum of Natural History in Washington, D.C., I was stopped in my tracks by a mineral. No, it didn't fall from the roof and hit me in the head. It was a cluster of pyrite standing in a glass case. When I first saw it, I thought it was a piece of modern sculpture. Each piece was a perfect, shiny cube with flat sides and straight edges, like dice made out of steel. The cubes were stuck together in a **swirly** tower formation. When I read the note on the case, I learned the structure wasn't man-made—these awesome shapes were natural!

Of Earth's 2,000 minerals, only about 100 are common. Common minerals include the silicates, such as quartz, which make up most of the rock on Earth. Another common mineral is one you eat every day—salt. Gold, silver, and gems are among Earth's rare minerals.

It's Elementary

Minerals are made of chemicals called **elements.** Everything on the planet, inorganic (nonliving) and organic, can be broken down into elements, which in turn can be broken down into *atoms*, the smallest unit of matter. (Atoms break down into all kinds of amazing things, such as quarks and antimatter, but basically, an atom is the smallest bit of matter before it turns into plain, good old energy.)

One hundred three elements have been identified. Of those 103 elements, only 8 are commonly found in rock. These 8 elements make up 98 percent of Earth's rocky crust. Of those 8, oxygen and silicon are the most common elements in

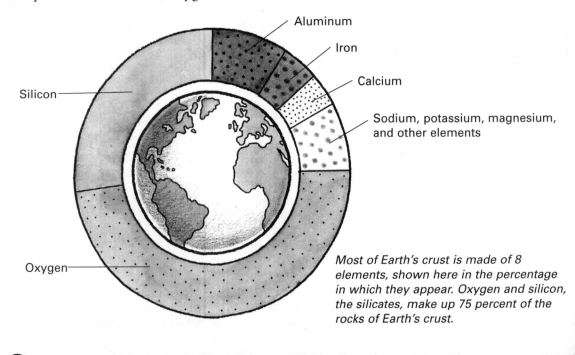

Aluminum

Iron

Calcium

Sodium, potassium, magnesium, and other elements

Silicon

Oxygen

Most of Earth's crust is made of 8 elements, shown here in the percentage in which they appear. Oxygen and silicon, the silicates, make up 75 percent of the rocks of Earth's crust.

rock, making up 75 percent of all rocks. These 2 elements combine to form the most common family of minerals, the **silicates.** Silicates are so common that, as far as geologists are concerned, there are two kinds of minerals: silicates and nonsilicates. The other elements that make up most of the minerals of Earth's crust are aluminum, iron, calcium, sodium, potassium, and magnesium.

Most minerals are made of more than one element. The combination of one or more elements is a **compound.** (The elements hydrogen and oxygen, for example, combine to form the compound we call water.) Most minerals are compounds that include oxygen and silicon. One exception is the mineral *diamond*, which is not a compound but made of only one element, carbon.

Mineralogists, scientists who study minerals, define a *mineral* as a substance that has all four of the following features:

1. Exists in nature (not made by humans)
2. Formed of inorganic materials, with some exceptions
3. Has atoms arranged in a regular pattern, forming solid units called **crystals**
4. Contains the same chemical makeup wherever it is found

In addition to the very common silicates, the **family tree** of common minerals includes the *carbonates*, all containing carbon and oxygen, including the common sedimentary rock limestone, which is made of calcite; the *oxides*, all containing oxygen, such as corundum, a compound of oxygen and aluminum; and the *sulfides*, all containing sulfur, such as galena, the mineral used to make pencil lead.

Crystals

toms in crystals are arranged in a special way that creates symmetry in the crystal. **Symmetry** means that each section of the crystal has a matching section on the opposite side. Imagine the atoms forming a room with walls, a ceiling, and a floor. Each of the flat surfaces is called a crystal's *face*. The "ceiling" face is like a mirror image of the "floor" face that lies opposite it. Each "wall" matches the wall

You're Salty!

People are made of minerals, too. Salt, a compound of the elements sodium and chlorine, is a very important mineral in the human body. The fluid that surrounds every cell in the body contains about 1/2 cup (89 ml) of salt, which is also one of the main ingredients of blood. You can taste salt in your tears, your sweat, and your blood.

opposite it. A crystal contains many of these rooms built on top of and around each other.

Crystals are divided into seven basic groups, based on their symmetry. The pyrite (also called "fool's gold" for its brassy, shiny appearance) that grabbed my attention at the museum is a mineral formed of *cubic*—cube-shaped—crystals. The *hexagonal* group contains crystals with six wall sides, as well as a top and a bottom; for instance, water's ice crystals are hexagonal snowflakes.

Crystal symmetry. The structure of crystals comes in seven varieties.

Orthorhombic (peridot)   Monoclinic (orthoclase)   Triclinic (axinite)

Cubic (diamond, garnet)   Trigonal (ruby, sapphire)

Tetragonal (zircon)   Hexagonal (emerald, aquamarine)

CRYSTALS YOU CAN GROW!

Many rocks and gemstones form out of mineral-rich **solutions** (liquids containing dissolved substances). You can create a quick-growing crystal garden using a homemade solution and a few common materials. **This activity includes some poisonous materials—you MUST have ADULT supervision!**

What You Need:
- Foil pie pan

- Newspaper

- Four or five rocks

- Charcoal briquette, broken into two or three pieces

- Spoon

- Water

- Liquid laundry bluing (available in the laundry-soap section of the supermarket, highly poisonous)

- Salt

- Household ammonia (highly poisonous)

- Glass jar or glass measuring cup

- Tablespoon measure

- Paper towels

- Magnifying glass (optional)

What to Do:
1. Place the foil pie pan on some newspaper (in case you spill).
2. Place the rocks and charcoal chunks in the pie plate.

continued

continued

3. Measure 3 tablespoons of water, 3 tablespoons of bluing, and 3 tablespoons of salt into the glass jar or measuring cup.
4. Mix together, stirring slowly.
5. Carefully add 1 tablespoon ammonia, and mix well. Keep the ammonia away from your face, eyes, and nose, as the fumes may irritate them. Put the cap back on the ammonia bottle.
6. Slowly spoon the solution onto the rocks and charcoal. Don't pour it, and try to prevent the solution from pooling into the bottom of the pan.
7. Use paper towels to wipe up any solution that may have spilled onto the table, floor, or anywhere else.
8. Set the pan aside for at least 24 hours.
9. Observe the crystal garden closely with a magnifying glass.

What Happens and Why:

The solution contains elements and minerals. As the water of the solution evaporates, the minerals group together in the form of crystals. Some minerals from the outer surface of the rock and the charcoal also mixed with the solution.

This is how minerals form out of the hot, thick solution called magma, as well as the liquid solution that separates from magma and forms special mineral deposits, called gems and ores (discussed later in this chapter).

A **crystal** is a nonliving object, but it forms over time in a pattern that makes it appear to grow. Atoms bond to the smooth, flat surfaces of the crystal's "rooms" and build up new layers. Layer by layer, the crystal grows larger. Mineral crystals come in a huge variety of sizes. Kaolin crystals are so tiny they can only be seen with a very powerful microscope. Quartz crystals, however, can grow to be several yards (meters) long and to weigh tons! Most minerals grow in liquids, including the very hot liquid magma found in Earth's mantle. When the magma moves up into the crust or out to the surface, it begins to cool. The cooling process makes some atoms bond together and form crystals.

Name That Mineral

Having trouble sorting out your mica from your feldspar? No problem! You don't need to measure out the angles of a mineral's crystals or put them under a gazillion-dollar electron microscope to identify them (although mineralogists love doing that sort of thing). Minerals can be identified by four main properties: color, luster, cleavage, and hardness.

Color. Some minerals give themselves away at first sight with an unmistakable color. Examples are bright-green malachite, yellow sulfur, and red cinnabar. Many minerals have similar coloring, however, and cannot be identified simply by looks alone.

A better color identification is made by using the **streak test.** The mineral is rubbed against a slightly rough piece

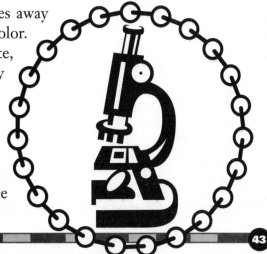

CRYSTALS GOOD ENOUGH TO EAT!

Sugar is another common crystal. Here, you can observe how it forms out of solution into pretty crystal formations. *Note:* The final step in this experiment is *tasty*!

What You Need:
- 4-inch (10-cm) piece of clean string

- Clean pencil

- Clean paper clip

- $\frac{1}{2}$ cup (125 ml) boiling water (requires adult supervision!)

- Saucepan

- $1\frac{1}{2}$ cups (375 ml) granulated sugar

- Spoon

- Glass measuring cup

- Food coloring

- Magnifying glass

What to Do:
1. Tie one end of the string to the middle of the pencil.
2. Tie the other end to the paper clip. Set aside.
3. With the help of an adult, bring the water to a boil in the saucepan. Ask the adult to remove the pan from the heat after it starts to boil.
4. Add the sugar to the water in the saucepan, and stir until the sugar dissolves (no sugar particles show).
5. Pour the solution into the glass measuring cup.
6. Stir in 3 drops of food coloring.
7. Place the pencil on top of the cup so that the paper clip dangles in the solution.

continued

continued

8. Set the cup aside in a place where it will not be disturbed. Watch it every day, but don't touch or shake the glass!
9. On the fourth day, carefully pour out the remaining water, and remove the crystals. Look closely at the crystals through a magnifying glass.
10. Pop a crystal into your mouth and enjoy!

What Happens and Why:
As the faces of the crystals float in the solution, they attach themselves to the faces of other crystals. Layer by layer, the tiny crystals build up into larger crystal formations in a regular pattern. You can see both the structure of individual sugar crystals and the larger structure with the aid of a magnifying glass. This is how minerals form out of the hot, thick solution called magma, as well as the liquid solution that separates from magma and forms gems and ores.

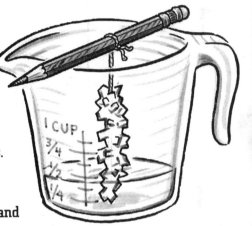

of white porcelain, such as the back side of enamel tile. Rubbing the mineral against the tile grinds the substance into a fine powder and leaves a telltale streak of color. The streak may be different than the color of the mineral.

Crystal Size: It's All in the Timing

When magma cools slowly deep in the earth, crystals have time to grow—sometimes into very large structures. In South Dakota, miners found a hunk of spodumene crystal (which looks similar to a column of clear quartz crystal) 47 feet (14 m) long and weighing 90 tons!

Crystals that cool very quickly, however, may not have time to form crystals at all. **Volcanic glass,** such as obsidian, is formed when minerals harden into a solid mass without a pattern of crystals.

EXPERIMENT

THE STREAK TEST

Discover the sometimes hidden color of minerals with the streak test. You can purchase inexpensive, labeled samples at a natural history museum gift shop, hobby shop, or rock shop.

What You Need:
- Mineral samples

- Porcelain tile (available at a hardware store)

What to Do:
1. Press down and slide each mineral sample along the rough back side of the tile.
2. Observe whether the streak is the same color as the sample.

What Happens and Why:
The true color of a mineral is revealed in the streak test. By rubbing the mineral against the tile, a small portion of the sample is ground into fine powder. The color of the powdery mineral is always the same, regardless of the outer appearance of the sample.

Hematite has a reddish-brown to black color but always leaves a red streak. Chalcopyrite is a yellow mineral that makes a green-black streak.

Luster. We see minerals, and any other object, because they *reflect* (bounce back) light to our eyes. The quality of a mineral's reflected light is called **luster.**

Flaky cleavage is found in minerals such as gypsum and mica. These minerals break apart in thin sheets along one plane.

Two-way-break cleavage creates steplike breaks in two directions.

Block break cleavage breaks minerals such as galena and halite into cubic blocks along three planes at right angles (45°) to each other.

Rhombic cleavage also breaks a mineral into three planes, but the angles are not right angles.

Minerals such as gold, ilmenite, and galena **shine** with a **metallic** (having a shiny, sparkling quality) luster. Some minerals with this brilliant, shiny luster are **opaque** (having a solid quality through which light cannot pass). Some minerals are **transparent**—objects can be seen through them as if they were clear glass. Transparent minerals include quartz, gypsum, and mica. Light also passes through **translucent** minerals, such as milky quartz, but they are not clear enough for objects to be seen through them. Talc has a *pearly* luster, and clay has a *dull* luster.

Cleavage. Many minerals break into pieces that have flat surfaces, or **planes.** This type of break, called **cleavage,** differs from breakage that is rough and splintery. Minerals that have cleavage—such as mica, halite, topaz, and diamond—break along smooth planes that reveal their crystal structure. Four common cleavage patterns are flaky, two-way-break, block-break, and rhombic cleavage.

Hardness. A mineral can also be identified by what will scratch it and what will not. Hardness is rated according to the Mohs' Hardness Scale, invented by German mineralogist Friedrich Mohs in 1812. The softest mineral, talc, is at the top, and the hardest, diamond, at the bottom of the scale. Each mineral in the scale can scratch the previous ones, and can be scratched by the ones following it. For example, quartz (7 on the scale) can scratch feldspar (6), but cannot scratch topaz (8). Topaz, however, can scratch quartz. Diamond is the hardest object on Earth and cannot be scratched by anything except another diamond.

The Mohs' Hardness Scale continues to be a popular clue to a mineral's identity. Common objects are used to test hardness, including your fingernail, which has a hardness of 2 on the scale.

Mohs' Hardness Scale

Hardness	Mineral	Hardness description	Common tests
1	Talc	Very Soft	Scratched by a fingernail
2	Gypsum	Very Soft/Soft	Scratched by a fingernail
3	Calcite	Soft	Scratched by a copper coin
4	Fluorite	Semihard	Scratched by an iron nail
5	Apatite	Hard	Scratched by glass
6	Feldspar	Hard	Scratched by penknife blade
7	Quartz	Very Hard	Scratched by a steel file
8	Topaz	Very Hard	Scratched by sandpaper
9	Corundum	Very Hard	(No everyday equivalent)
10	Diamond	Very Hard (4 million times harder than the softest talc!)	(No everyday equivalent; scratched only by diamond)

THE SCRATCH TEST

"Hard as a rock" doesn't mean much if you're talking about soft rocks such as talc, which used to be an ingredient in baby powder! Test out the hardness of your own mineral samples, using the standard of the Mohs' Hardness Scale.

What You Need:
- Mineral samples

- Penny

- Iron nail

- Penknife (use only with adult supervision!)

What to Do:
1. Scratch each sample with your finger-nail. If it does not leave a scratch, the mineral is 3 or harder.
2. Scratch the 3 or harder minerals with the penny. If it does not leave a scratch, the mineral is 4 or harder.
3. Scratch the 4 or harder minerals with the nail. If it does not leave a scratch, the mineral is 5 or harder.
4. With an adult's supervision, scratch the 5 or harder minerals with a penknife. If it does not leave a scratch, the mineral is 7 or harder.

What Happens and Why:
The Mohs' Hardness Scale identifies minerals by their ability to scratch or be scratched by other minerals. Testing each sample according to the scale will show the hardness of the mineral, according to this standard scale.

Crystal Garden

Some igneous rocks form into a round shape with liquid in the center. As the liquid squeezes out of the cooling magma, it leaves a hollow space in the rock. In this rock structure, called a **geode**, crystals form on the inside wall of the rock, pointing into the hollow space. Cut in half to expose the crystals within, a geode looks like a magical crystal garden.

A geode is a rock in which crystals form inside a hollow center.

Gemstones

The superstars of the mineral world are gemstones, prized for thousands of years for their beauty and ability to last a long time. **Gemstones** are hard minerals that form under special conditions, when magma beneath the crust produces minerals that are *dazzling* in shape and color.

Sometimes, as magma cools and forms igneous rock, the liquid part of the magma is squeezed out of the solid part, which hardens into pegmatite rock. *Pegmatite*, a type of granite, is the intrusive igneous rock from which gems are formed. Gas also escapes from the magma and forms gas pockets in the crust. The liquid seeps into the cracks and openings in the crust made by the gas. Floating (dissolved) in the liquid are minerals from the original magma. Liquid containing dissolved substances, such as minerals, is known as a *solution*. As the liquid slowly evaporates, the minerals group together, or *crystallize*, in magnificent crystal formations. In this way, gemstones form from a liquid solution that is *squeezed* out of magma deep in the Earth.

Gems make up a very small portion of Earth's crust and only appear near the surface when **powerful** forces lift them from below. These forces include mountain building and volcanic eruptions. For example, rubies and jade were brought to the surface with the Himalayan Mountains in Nepal and Tibet. In Thailand, lava eruptions carried garnets, rubies, and sapphires to the surface; people then discovered these gems within the basalt rock formed from the lava.

Diamond, the hardest mineral, is named from the Greek word *adamas*, "unconquerable." Diamond is formed of the element carbon and crystallizes in an igneous rock called kimberlite. This rock is named after Kimberley, South Africa, where a **huge** column of kimberlite has roots 200 miles (320 km) deep. All diamonds are valuable, either as gemstones or for drills and other industrial uses.

Rubies are the most rare and valuable gemstones on Earth—beating out even top-quality diamonds. They are the red variety of the mineral corundum. Corundum is the second-hardest mineral on Earth, making rubies very hard and long-lasting. A fine ruby has an intense red color that looks like glowing coal. The very word *red* comes from "ruber," Latin for ruby.

Corundum also forms blue crystals, called **sapphires.** The **most** famous and valuable sapphires are a deep, rich blue that earns this gem the name "gem of the heavens." The ancient Persians believed that the blue color of the sky was reflected off a giant

Great Shades!

Roman Emperor Nero (A.D. 37–68) wore emerald sunglasses while he watched the gladiators fight in the Colosseum!

Gem Cutting

Gemstones go through a very delicate cutting and polishing process before arriving at the jewelry store or the museum. The art of cutting gemstones has been practiced for thousands of years. Two main types of cuts are used to display the special qualities of each gem. The simplest and oldest method of cutting is called the **cabochon,** in which the gem is formed and polished into a smooth, rounded shape. The second type of cut is called the **faceted cut,** which became popular in medieval Europe and is still used today. With a faceted cut, a gem is shaped into a pattern of highly polished, flat planes that act as mirrors. Light leaps off each plane of transparent and translucent gems and also bounces off the mirrorlike planes inside the stone. This brilliant display of light creates an effect known as the "fire" of a gem. If a gem is cut poorly, the light does not create a special flash, and the gem loses value.

sapphire upon which Earth rested. A very rare type of sapphire, the star sapphire, contains tiny, needle-like grains in a six-rayed star formation.

Beryl is the mineral that produces **emerald,** the highly prized, rich green gem. Some of the finest emeralds in the world are in the British Crown Jewels, which are on display in the Tower of London. When I visited this collection, I learned why people have such a powerful attraction to gemstones. Each face of the emeralds sparkled with a green that is brighter and more intense than the green of trees and plants.

Emeralds were also the favorite gem of Queen Cleopatra of Egypt (69–30 B.C.). Her emerald mines, first discovered in the year 1650 B.C., were rediscovered about 100 years ago. The mines still contained a fascinating collection of ancient mining tools, but no more emeralds. The mummies of ancient Egypt were often buried with an emerald necklace, as the green of the emerald was a symbol for eternal youth.

Opals contain tiny bits of rainbow-colored silica within a solid "body" color. The body color can be milky, clear, gray, or black, as in the gem's most precious form, black opal. The shiny bits of silica twinkle with blue, green, yellow, and red colors. Opals form in sedimentary rocks, as well as in gas cavities in igneous rocks.

Quartz rock crystal is considered *semiprecious* because it is not as rare as other gemstones. Even though it is more common, it is a very beautiful gem that appears in a wide variety of shapes and colors. Ancient people thought that quartz rock crystal, which is clear like glass, was ice that had frozen so hard it could not thaw. The word *crystal* comes from the Greek word *kryos*, "icy cold."

Quartz rock crystal was used thousands of years ago to make *crystal balls*, which were believed to be clear enough to look into the future. (Today, pure, spotless quartz rock crystal is difficult to find, and the crystal balls found in gift shops are made out of glass.) Some of the colorful types of quartz are purple or violet amethyst, orange citrine, rose and smoky quartz, tigereye, striped agate, bloodstone, jasper, and black onyx.

Metals

Liquid and gas rising out of magma also produce hard and shiny solids called **metals.** The very hot, mineral-rich liquid or gas squeezes into cracks, where it cools. Minerals solidify along the walls of the cracks, forming branchlike **veins** within the crust. Lead, zinc, copper, iron, silver, and gold are some of the metals formed in veins of rock. Metals are usually mixed with other elements, forming a solid known as an **ore.** Before the metal can be used, it must be separated from the ore.

Gold is often found attached to quartz, either in veins or in gravel and sand deposits. The quartz/gold ore is crushed to separate the precious metal from the rock. Soft and easy to shape into jewelry, gold reflects light with a shiny, yellow brilliance that no other metal can match. These qualities have made gold a valuable mineral for thousands of years.

In addition to being used for jewelry, gold has also been fashioned into coins throughout history. Gold coins are very impressive. I can still remember when my fourth-grade teacher brought some historic gold coins to class. They were gold doubloons from the 1600s, which had been found in a sunken pirate ship! Even today, gold is used as a *standard* (the basis of value) for money, in the form of gold bars.

Many other metals are valuable, too. Life wouldn't be the same without the metals that ores provide. Copper and aluminum are good *conductors of electricity* (electrical current can

From Airplanes to Drumstick Wrap!

Aluminum foil, the thin, easy-to-fold metal you use to wrap up leftovers, was invented by Mr. Reynolds after World War II. He created the household product out of tons of scrap metal from the war's leftover airplanes.

easily pass through them). Copper is often used for electrical wiring, and it is easy to shape into useful objects such as water pipes. Aluminum is lightweight and is used for power lines, food cans, pots and pans, cars, washing machines, and many other useful things.

Iron, a very **strong** metal, is the main ingredient in *steel*, a mixture of metals that is used in building. A network of steel beams is called the "skeleton" of a modern building—there would be no skyscrapers without steel.

Silver is a popular metal for jewelry and is also used in photography. Cameras contain a silver plate that bounces light onto the film and creates an image.

Platinum is a metal even more valuable than gold or silver. Unlike silver, platinum does not *tarnish* (discolor) easily. This silver-colored metal is used to make jewelry and mechanical, electrical, and scientific instruments.

Metals are valued for their ability to be pressed into different shapes without breaking. This quality is called the **malleability** of a metal. Earth's most malleable metal is gold, with silver and platinum the second and third most malleable. Gold can be pounded into an extremely thin, featherlight sheet called **gold leaf,** which is used to decorate art objects, furniture, and buildings. Pounded by machine, as well as by hand, the first step in making gold leaf is to pound a small piece of gold into a square of gold foil. The foil is placed between special papers

The World's Oldest Mineral

The oldest minerals ever found are zircon crystals discovered in the Jack Hills, 430 miles (688 km) north of Perth in western Australia. *Zircon* is a silicate mineral, and these pieces were dated to be 4.276 billion years old. Unlike the oldest rocks on Earth, found in Canada, these are only flecks of minerals and are no longer grouped together to form rocks.

and pounded many times. The pounding presses the foil into a sheet that is only 1/4,000 of an inch (1/100,000 mm) thick!

The Sky Is Falling!

ROCKS FROM SPACE

The nights were very dark where I grew up in the Virginia countryside. There were no city lights to cover up the star-filled sky. One night, when I was about seven years old, I saw a star dart toward Earth with a bright white streak. My parents told me that it was a shooting star, and that every time I saw one I should make a wish. Years later, one of my wishes came true when I had the opportunity to *touch* a shooting star that had fallen to Earth and was put on display at a museum!

Shooting stars are **meteors,** rocks from space. When a meteor enters Earth's *atmosphere* (a layer of gases, including the oxygen we breathe), it rubs against the atoms of gas and gets hot. The heat is caused by **friction,** the same force that heats up the palms of your hands when you rub them together a few times. Many meteors get so hot that they burn up completely in a streak of light—which is commonly called a *shooting star* or a *falling star*. Most meteors range in size from a dust particle to a rock that would fit in your hand.

Meteors usually burn up about 30 miles (50 km) above the Earth. A larger meteor that **burns** very brightly is called a **fireball.** On October 5, 1996, a fireball flew over New Mexico and California and was described by witnesses as fiery red with sparks coming from it, trailing a flaming yellow tail.

Fireworks from Space!
The World's Largest Meteor Shower

The largest meteor shower on record occurred on the night of November 16–17, 1966, when a group called the Leonid meteors streaked through the sky. The meteor shower was observed between western North America and eastern Russia. At the height of the shower, meteors were spotted over Arizona at a rate of 2,300 per minute for a period of 20 minutes! Scientists call a rare event such as the Leonid meteor shower, with more than 1,000 meteors seen per minute, a *meteor storm.*

Daytime Meteors

Meteors enter Earth's atmosphere during the daylight hours, too, but we cannot see them. Sunlight is brighter than the meteor and prevents our viewing them. The exception is the rare sighting of a large fireball during the day.

On August 10, 1972, for example, a very bright daylight fireball appeared in the skies of the western United States and Canada. At about 3:30 in the afternoon, tourists in the Yellowstone, Grand Teton, and Glacier national parks snapped pictures as a glowing object sped across the sky from south to north, leaving a smoky trail. Scientists believe that the fireball did not land, but passed out of the atmosphere and returned to space. If it had landed, it would have released as much energy as a nuclear bomb!

A meteor that survives the hot ride through Earth's atmosphere and drops to Earth is called a **meteorite.** About 19,000 meteorites land on Earth every year. Most land in the ocean or in areas where few people live, and the meteorites become lost forever. A very few, however—about five per year—are discovered in or near towns or cities.

Meteorites take a beating when they fall through Earth's atmosphere! Friction melts and sweeps away some of the outer surface of the rock. The melted patch later hardens into a dark, thin layer called **fusion crust.**

Sometimes Earth passes through a cluster of meteors as it orbits around the Sun. This causes a **meteor shower,** in which many meteors (shooting stars) appear every hour.

Meteorite Origins

Most meteorites come from the **asteroid belt,** a group of solid, rocklike objects, which revolves around the sun in the large space between the orbits of Mars and Jupiter. The asteroid belt contains more than 100,000 **asteroids,** objects that

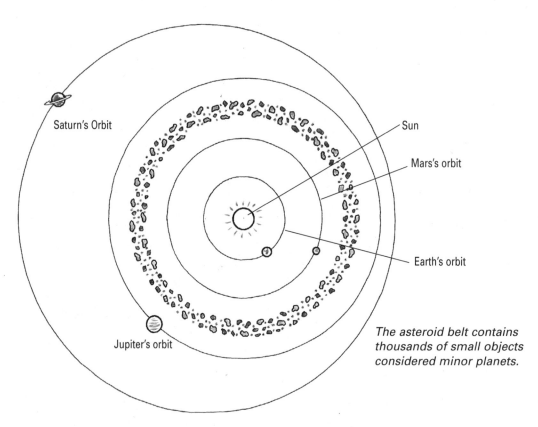

Saturn's Orbit

Sun

Mars's orbit

Earth's orbit

Jupiter's orbit

The asteroid belt contains thousands of small objects considered minor planets.

measure between 0.6 miles (1 km) and 62 miles (100 km) across. They are the remains of larger objects that collided with each other and broke up.

Asteroids are actually minor planets, and more than 3,000 of the largest ones have been given names. The largest is Ceres, which measures 620 miles (1,000 km) in *diameter* (the length of a straight line through the center of the sphere). The smallest named asteroid, called 1993KA2, has a diameter of about 16 feet (4.8 m).

Like Earth, asteroids are formed of layers containing a core, a mantle, and an outer crust. When asteroids collide with each other, pieces can bounce out of the asteroid belt's orbit and can travel to other parts of the solar system—including Earth—where they may fall as meteorites.

The Hubbell telescope, a mind-boggling power-house of a telescope that orbits Earth, recently provided a close-up of Vesta, the third-largest asteroid. In May 1997, the Hubbell picture revealed a huge *crater* (a huge dent in the crust, created by the impact of a meteor) on Vesta. Scientists calculated that the crater was formed when a space rock about 19 miles (31 km) wide hit Vesta at a speed of 11,000 miles an hour (17,710 km/h).

Scientists had already figured out the chemical makeup of Vesta. It turns out that about 6 percent of the meteorites on Earth have a makeup that matches the chemistry of Vesta, which means that these meteorites came from Vesta. The Hubbell picture confirmed that a huge collision, several billion years ago, tore a huge part of Vesta apart and sent rocks *flying* into space—and to Earth.

Meteorites also come from the Moon and from Mars. When a large meteorite strikes the Moon or Mars, the collision breaks off pieces of the planet or the Moon and sends it out into space. Some of those pieces land on Earth as meteorites.

Scientists think that some meteorites may come from **comets.** Like asteroids and the major planets, comets are

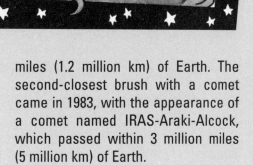

Comet Facts

Most famous comet: Halley's comet orbits around the Sun once every 76 years. Confirmed sightings of the comet have been recorded since 240 B.C. The comet is named after Edmund Halley (1656–1742), an English scientist who suggested that the comet appears on a regular timetable. Halley's comet last appeared, right on schedule, in 1986. Its next appearance will be in the year 2061. How old will you be when Halley's comet appears?

Closest comet to Earth: In 1770, Lexell's comet came within 745,000 miles (1.2 million km) of Earth. The second-closest brush with a comet came in 1983, with the appearance of a comet named IRAS-Araki-Alcock, which passed within 3 million miles (5 million km) of Earth.

Longest comet tail: The great comet of 1843 dazzled the world with a tail that trailed for 205 million miles (328 million km).

The Comet of a Lifetime

American author Mark Twain was born in a year that Halley's comet appeared, 1835, and he died in the year of its next appearance, 1910.

objects that orbit around the sun, but they are not made of solid rock. Comets come from the outer limits of the solar system, far beyond the planets, and they are made of icy debris that has been floating about for billions of years. Comets contain a solid **nucleus** (center) formed of dust, ice, and chemicals. The comet is surrounded by a cloud of dust and gas that forms a tail when the comet nears the Sun. The **solar wind** (particles of energy flowing from the Sun) blows the comet dust into a long, streaming tail. The rarest type of meteorites, such as the Murchison meteorite that fell onto Australia in 1969, contains mixtures of carbon and water, similar to the contents of a comet. Only about 3 out of every 100 meteorites seen to fall are of this type.

When a star falls from the sky

It leaves a fiery trail. It does not die.

Its shade goes back to its own place to shine again.

The Indians sometimes find the small stars

where they have fallen in the grass.

Menomini Legend
(Native Americans from the Great Lakes region)

Types of Meteorites

Alien rocks (that's what I like to call meteorites) that fall from the sky are rare, and they're a hot collector's item. Before 1969, there were only about 2,000 known meteorites. Then, an exciting discovery in Antarctica led the way to uncovering more than 10,000 new meteorites. A Japanese scientific team discovered a section of ice containing a large group of meteorites frozen to the surface of the ice. The meteorites fell to Earth between 100,000 and 1 million years ago; they have been perfectly preserved, slightly embedded in the ice. The dark meteorites, grouped in clusters, are easy to find on the snow-free ice. They piled up in clusters when the slowly moving glacial ice moved against an obstacle, such as a rock. The meteorites were scraped off the ice and gathered up around the rock. The Antarctic discovery is important to scientists because meteorites contain clues to the elements that joined together to form the entire solar system, including planet Earth.

There are three main types of meteorites: stones, irons, and stony-irons. **Stones** are the most commonly found meteorites. They are the closest in structure to Earth rocks, often containing the minerals olivine and pyroxene. One

World's Biggest Hands-on Meteorite

The largest meteorite on display for viewing and touching is Cape York, now displayed in the Hall of Meteorites at the American Museum of Natural History in New York City. This is where my wish came true and I first touched a meteorite. Cape York is a huge, smooth, black rock weighing 68,000 pounds, or 34 tons (30,600 kg; 30 metric tons).

famous stony meteorite is Barwell, which fell at Barwell, England, on Christmas Eve in 1965. (All meteorites are named after the places where they fall.) Barwell is 4.6 billion years old, giving it the same birthday as Earth because it formed at the same time, although somewhere else in the solar system.

Meteorites such as Barwell come from the crust layer of an asteroid. Some stony meteorites are easily identified as alien rocks because they contain small, beadlike objects scientists call *chondrules*, which are not found in Earth rocks. The minerals in chondrules are arranged in a unique way, probably the result of being melted when objects collided with them.

Irons are meteorites made primarily of the elements iron and nickel. They are more rare than stony meteorites, and they come from the central core of an asteroid. Iron meteorites are very heavy. The largest known meteorite is an iron from Africa, named Hoba, which weighs about 60 tons (55 metric tons)! Hoba was found in 1920

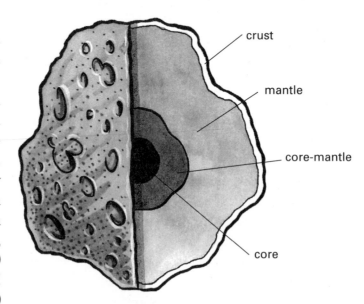

Most meteorites come from pieces of broken asteroids. Stony meteorites come from the crust, iron meteorites come from the core, and stony-irons come from the core-mantle.

and is a block 9 feet (2.7 m) long by 8 feet (2.4 m) wide.

Stony-irons, as the name implies, are meteorites containing a mixture of stone and iron. Many stony-irons are among the meteorites discovered in the Antarctic ice. With rich greenish crystals set in bright metal, stony-irons are the most beautiful meteorites. A stony-iron meteorite from Argentina, called the Esquel, has been described as "the most beautiful meteorite in the world," and a small sample of it costs nearly $30,000! Stony-irons are formed from the core–mantle of an asteroid, the part-solid, part-molten rock layer that surrounds the central core.

Of the 17,000 known meteorites, 11 have been identified as rocks from the moon, and 11 as rocks from Mars. Most meteorites are from asteroids and are about the same age as Earth, around 4.5 billion years old. The meteorites from the Moon and Mars, however, are younger. Moon meteorites are less than 4 billion years old, and some Mars meteorites have been dated to be only about 1.3 billion years old. The age of these meteorites proves that they did not come from asteroids, but formed on a moon or planet that had, at some time in its history, made new rock.

The *lunar* (meaning from the Moon) meteorites can also be compared to the Moon rocks collected and brought back to Earth by the Apollo mission astronauts. They look very similar and contain the same minerals.

In addition to their age, meteorites from Mars may contain another clear clue to their origin. Inside one of these meteorites, scientists found some trapped gas. When they analyzed the gas, they found it to be nearly identical to the atmosphere on Mars.

Moon Rocks

American astronauts walked on the Moon six times and carried a collection of Moon rocks to Earth on every return trip. The Russian space program

sent three crewless missions to the Moon, which brought back Moon rocks, too. Scientists have learned a lot about the Moon by studying the makeup of Moon rocks.

The Moon contains two basic types of rocks. The rocks found on the *mare areas*—the dark, smooth landscapes—were created from great lava flows. These Moon rocks are called **mare basalts** and are similar to the basalt rock of Earth. Mare basalts formed when molten lava flowed through huge cracks in the Moon's crust and hardened into rock. Dark gray or brownish gray, a mare basalt rock has tiny holes on the surface, which look like craters. These tiny holes, called **zap pits,** were made when fast-moving meteorites, smaller than a grain of sand, crashed into the rock.

The other type of Moon rock is found on the highland areas. It is made of a complex mixture of pieces of crushed rock that has been melted, crushed, and melted again many times from meteorite collisions. In appearance, these rocks are similar to breccias, Earth rocks that have been mixed and cemented together. The minerals that make up the Moon rocks from the highlands are feldspar, olivine, pyroxene, and ilmenite.

The entire surface of the Moon is covered with a thin layer of tiny rocks called a **regolith,** which averages from 15 to 30 feet (5 to 10 m) deep. Unlike the soil of Earth, the regolith contains no moisture and no decaying plant or animal remains. The tiny rocks that make up the regolith are smaller than 1/25 of an inch (less than 1 mm) across. The regolith formed from meteorite impacts that crashed over the Moon's surface for 3 or 4 billion years, smashing all the surface rock to bits.

Some of the tiny rocks are actually beads of bright orange, yellow, and green glass. The glass forms when a meteorite hits the surface and melts some of the Moon rock through the heat of the collision. A drop of melted rock flies into the air and cools immediately into glass. This is similar to volcanic rocks on Earth, which also cool quickly to form glassy rocks, such as obsidian.

Mars Rocks

As I write this, Mars rocks are front-page news all over the world. On the Fourth of July 1997, the Pathfinder spacecraft landed on Mars. Shortly afterward, three panels from the spacecraft unfolded, and a small robot named Sojourner wheeled out onto the surface. Sojourner is only 1 foot (30.5 cm) tall and 2 feet (61 cm) long—about the size of a skateboard—but it carries some very high-tech equipment. Cameras take both black-and-white and color photographs and send them back to Earth. For the first time, people on Earth have been able to see sweeping images of the dusty, dry, and red Mars landscape.

One of Sojourner's first amazing pictures showed Mars soil, gravel-size rocks, boulders, and a line of small hills in the distance. Within weeks, scientists discovered that dozens of Mars rocks have two colors: red and blue. The blue sides of the rocks are facing the wind, while the red sides have the rusty red color of the soil. The wind probably

Life on Mars?
A Meteorite May Hold the Clues!

In August 1996, NASA made an announcement that rocked the world. Scientists stated that a meteorite from Mars contained markings that may be fossils (imprints) of microscopic organisms that lived on Mars more than 3 billion years ago. The evidence is being studied by a new group of scientists. If it is proved that simple life forms existed on Mars, the finding will spark many new questions. Is there still microscopic life on that planet? If not, what happened to the ancient life forms? Will the rock studies done by the new Pathfinder mission provide even more clues?

wears away the red layer of rock, exposing an underlying section of the rock, which is blue.

Sojourner also carries a device called an Alpha proton x-ray spectrometer, which "sniffs" rocks and soil to analyze the chemical makeup of Mars rock for the first time. The x-ray device peers inside the rocks to identify chemicals and minerals. Scientists were surprised to find a 𝖒𝖚𝖈𝖍 higher silica content in one Mars rock than they expected. (Silica is found in Earth's igneous rocks.) This reveals that there was more heating and recycling of the Mars crust than scientists had previously assumed.

Scientists quickly named some of the rocks that showed up in Sojourner's photographs, using names that described what the rocks looked like: Barnacle Bill, Chimp, Yogi, Scooby Doo, the Bookshelf, Shark, Half-Dome, Moe, Stimpy, and Squid.

Rocks That Bomb

On the Moon, there's a huge *crater* (dented pit made by a meteorite) called Copernicus, surrounded by a starburst of light-colored rock that stretches out over the darker lava plain. When a meteorite hit

The Crater and the Dinosaurs

Earth's crust shows evidence of huge meteorite collisions. The largest crater on the planet lies on the Yucatan Peninsula of Mexico and may explain why the dinosaurs suddenly disappeared from Earth. Scientists estimate that the 186-mile (300-km) -wide crater was formed by a meteorite that crashed to Earth about 65 million years ago. The meteorite, originally an asteroid, would have kicked up billions of tons of dust and other material upon impact. Scientists believe the dust remained in Earth's atmosphere for about six months, blocking out the sunlight and causing temperatures all over the world to drop to near freezing.

Without sunlight, most plants would not have survived, and dinosaurs would have lost their food supply—if they hadn't already died from the cold. The date of this impact lines up with the period in which dinosaurs and many other animals and plants on Earth became extinct.

Fireball from Space!

On June 30, 1908, a massive explosion occurred in Siberia, Russia, which was probably caused by a meteorite. After examining the size of the crater, scientists calculated that a meteorite measuring 100 feet (30 m) in diameter exploded 33,000 feet (9,900 m) above ground. The speed of the meteorite created so much friction that the fireball exploded in the atmosphere, but close enough to the ground to create a lot of damage. The blast made shock waves that were felt 620 miles (992 km) away. The force of the explosion also flattened trees over an area of 1,500 square miles (3,900 square km) surrounding the crater.

the Moon to pound out that crater, it must have made a Moon-shaking blast! The Moon gets blasted by meteors much more often than Earth does, because the Moon has no atmosphere in which small meteorites can burn up.

Nearly all the objects in the solar system—including planets, **satellites** (objects that move in an orbit around a larger object) such as our Moon, and asteroids—have craters. Like the Moon, Mars has many more craters than Earth has. Most of the craters are found in Mars's *southern hemisphere* (the bottom half of the planet) because lava flows and other changes in the crust have erased the ones in the northern hemisphere. Craters on Mars show signs of weathering. Over billions of years, dust storms wear away the sharp edges of the crater rims and fill the bowls with sand. This makes the craters on Mars less rugged looking than Moon craters. Moon craters do not smooth down from weathering for one simple reason—there's no weather on the Moon! Without an atmosphere, there are no weather events such as wind or rain.

A famous crater closer to home is the Barringer Crater near Winslow, Arizona. This well-preserved crater was made by a massive iron–nickel asteroid about 27,000 years ago. The crater stretches 4,150 feet (1,265 m) across and dips down 575 feet (175 m) into the earth. Lining the circular crater like a fence is a jagged row of rock that rises from 130 to 155 feet (40 to 47 m) above the ground. (You

simple crater

complex crater

A simple crater is formed like a smooth bowl. In a complex crater, the crust rebounds up into a hill shape after a very powerful impact from a meteorite.

can see some great views of this crater in the final scene of the movie *Starman*, starring Jeff Bridges.)

The craters of Earth are continually being erased by erosion, being covered by volcanic eruptions, and being recycled into Earth's crust. Today, only 120 craters can be found on the planet. What happened to the meteorites that formed these craters? In many cases, the meteorite doesn't survive the impact with Earth. Upon **crashing** into the crust at great speed, the meteorite explodes and disintegrates into tiny dust fragments.

Two types of craters are formed by large meteorites. A **simple crater** consists of a smooth, bowl-shaped dent. The rock beneath the crater is broken in a special way by the impact, creating cracks called **shatter cones.** In a **complex crater,** the impact is so powerful that the earth at the bottom of the crater springs

Good Luck or Bad? Meteor Myths

Many of us have heard about the tradition of making a wish when we see a falling star. Throughout the world, people have developed beliefs about meteors.

• In medieval times, people in southwest Germany believed that a shooting star signaled one year of good fortune.

• Modern Hawaiian-Japanese people have the custom of opening the collar of their kimonos to admit the good luck of a meteor.

• In the Philippines, shooting stars are considered bad luck. It is traditional to ward off the bad luck of a shooting star by tying a knot in a handkerchief before the light fades out.

• In Chile, they are considered bad luck, too, but immediately picking up a stone is believed to protect a person from the bad luck of a meteor.

back up. This rebound rock takes the shape of a hill inside the crater. On the Moon, complex craters contain mountains created in this way.

Meteorites do more than punch dents in Earth. The heat of a meteorite collision melts some of the rock of Earth's crust at the crash site. Small blobs of molten rock fly out from the impact site and harden into a glossy, smooth rock called a **tektite** (from the Greek word *tektos*, meaning "molten"). Tektites are dark brown, green, or black in color.

5

Dinosaurs in Your Backyard

The World of Fossils

It's a typically frosty winter day in eastern Siberia. The year is 1901. A team of huskies pulls a sled carrying a few scientific explorers. Suddenly the dogs stop at a strange dark patch in the snow. The scientists brush away the snow to reveal the frozen body of a woolly mammoth. *Mammoths*, ancient ancestors of the elephants, became **extinct** (died out as a species) about 10,000 years ago. While digging their amazing find out of the frozen ground, the scientists discovered that the mammoth was

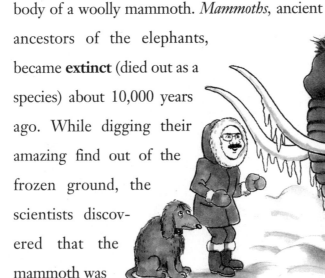

perfectly preserved. Unswallowed food was found in its mouth, and clotted blood in its chest. By this time, the **sled dogs** could smell the meat of the animal and were barking like crazy. The scientists tossed a few pieces of the red, newly thawed mammoth meat to the hungry dogs. The dogs thought it was delicious—even though it was the oldest dog food in history!

Everything we know about the early history of life on Earth we have learned from fossils. **Fossils** are the remains or traces of a living thing (from the Latin word *fossilis*, "dug up"). The Siberian mammoth is a rare type of fossil because it contains actual tissue of the animal. In most fossils, only the hard parts are preserved, such as shells or bones. **Paleontology** is the study of extinct life forms.

How Fossils Form

Nature preserves fossils in seven ways:

1. *Unaltered remains.* The mammoth found in Siberia is a classic example of this type of fossil preservation. Ice preserved the entire animal—skin, teeth, bones, and internal organs—before decay could set in. In addition to ice, animals have been preserved in thick, swampy bogs or in pools of oil like the famous La Brea Tar Pits in Los Angeles, California.

    The tar pits were formed when oil seeped up from cracks in the earth. Natural oil (crude oil) is made out of the remains of dead plants that are crushed on the bottom of seabeds over millions of years. When the oily plant material reaches high temperatures deep in the earth, the oil separates from the other plant material. The oil that came to the surface in California became thick tar because the light part of the oil evaporated in the open air. Animals that wandered—or were chased—into the thick, sticky tar were trapped and could not escape.

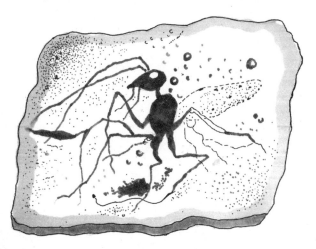

The La Brea Tar Pits contain the remains of thousands of animals that lived from 40,000 to 8,000 years ago. The extinct fossils include mammoths, mastodons (elephantlike mammals), and saber-toothed cats. Oil pools are found in other countries, too. In Poland, entire bodies of extinct woolly rhinoceroses are preserved in oil pits similar to the La Brea Pits.

Whole insects have also been preserved in the fossilized sap of ancient trees. An insect that got **trapped** in the sap long ago would end up being sealed in when the liquid sap hardened into a solid called **amber.** Amber, with or without insects or plants visible in it, is often worn as jewelry.

2. *Mineralization.* This process occurs when minerals fill up the tiny holes in an object's shell, bones, or other hard parts. The mineral matter hardens in the shape of the organism. When the minerals and the organic material both remain, this process is called *mineralization.*

3. *Replacement.* When the original organic substance (shell or bone) is dissolved and replaced by minerals, the process is called *replacement.* The dissolving and replacement processes happen so **slowly** that an exact copy of the original is made. Replacement is one of the most common ways fossils are made. Petrified wood, described in Chapter 2, is a common example of a fossil formed by the replacement method. Dinosaur bones are also petrified through replacement.

4. *Distillation.* This process occurs with objects such as the leaves of plants and trees, and with animal skin. These organisms are largely made of carbon, hydrogen, and oxygen.

Ōtzi and the Tollund Man

Perhaps the most fascinating of all unaltered remains are those of human beings. In 1991, two German hikers found the body of a man frozen in a glacier in the Otztal Alps. The 5,300-year-old man, known as Otzi, was probably a hunter or a trader who died in a snowstorm.

In 1950, a 2,000-year-old, perfectly preserved body, called Tollund man, was found in the Tollund Globin peat bog in Denmark. A *peat bog* is a spongy, thick layer of Earth containing dead plants and moist, mossy plants.

When the leaf or other object is covered by other materials until it becomes buried, chemical actions sweep away the hydrogen and oxygen until only a **thin** film of carbon remains. A stone carrying this type of fossil holds the black impression of a leaf or of the skin of a fish or other animals.

5. *Molds and imprints.* Sometimes, sediment hardens around an organic object. The object dissolves, leaving a dent in the rock that is the exact shape of the object. This is called a **fossil mold.** Pressing wax or clay into the mold will create a *cast* (statue) of the object. Molds of thin objects such as leaves are called **imprints.**

Some fossils form as an indentation called a mold.

6. *Footprints and trails.* The tracks of dinosaurs, lizards, early human beings, and other animals provide a lot of information about ancient life forms. Footprints can

reveal the size, shape, and habits of an animal. Trails show patterns of travel and feeding. Dinosaur footprints tell scientists whether the animal walked on two legs or four, whether it was fast-moving or slow, and whether it ran or hopped.

7. *Coprolites.* Don't tell anybody, but paleontologists like to look at dino poop! Scientists call it **coprolite,** excrement preserved in fossils. A great deal can be learned about an organism's diet and digestive system by studying coprolites. Even tiny insect coprolites reveal information about prehistoric plant life.

The Fossil Record

The scientific study of fossils began with the work of William Smith in England. As we learned in Chapter 1, Smith's great accomplishment was to identify that a specific type of fossil occurs at one specific time in history. The youngest fossils are found in the rock layers closest to the surface. The time in which the fossils lived grows more distant as you descend into deeper layers of rock.

Although Smith discovered the relationship between rocks and fossils, he could not put specific dates to his findings. In the nineteenth century, geologists could only refer to rocks and fossils as living "before" or "after" other rocks and fossils. This is dating in terms of **relative time.**

The dating of rocks and fossils in terms of actual years, or **absolute time,** was made possible with the discovery of radioactivity. French *physicist* (a scientist who studies matter and energy) Antoine-Henri Becquerel (1852–1908) discovered radioactivity in 1896. **Radioactivity** is a natural process by which certain elements change themselves into different elements, over a set rate of time. Scientists soon used this precisely timed feature to develop a system of radioactive dating of rocks. Every element contains its own "atomic clock," and scientists can read the clocks inside a rock to determine its age. They can then estimate the age of a fossil buried in that rock.

MAKE A FOSSIL MOLD

Create your own fossil mold! Using your choice of fossil, you can preserve the fossil image in a rocklike substance.

What You Need:
• "Fossil" (This can be anything you choose, such as a snail or other shell, a coin, or even a small plastic dinosaur!)

• Petroleum jelly

• Package of plaster of Paris

• Water

• Mixing bowl

• Spoon

• Saucer

What to Do:
1. Coat the fossil with petroleum jelly so that it will not stick to the plaster.
2. Coat the top side of the saucer with petroleum jelly.
3. Mix the plaster of Paris and water, enough to make about 1 cup (250 ml), according to the directions on the package.
4. Fill the saucer with the gooey plaster of Paris.
5. Place your fossil into the plaster, leaving enough of it exposed so that you can remove it. If you want to make an impression of the front of your fossil, place the front side into the plaster.
6. Put the saucer aside, and let the plaster harden for about five hours (or according to the directions on the package).
7. Remove your fossil from the hard plaster, and remove the mold from the saucer.

What Happens and Why:
When the plaster hardens, it molds around the shape of the fossil. Once the fossil is removed, the impression remains. This is what can happen when an organism is buried in sedimentary rock. The organism usually dissolves over time, and only the impression remains.

MAKE A FOSSIL CAST

Use the mold you've just created to make a *fossil cast*—a reproduction of the fossil that left the original impression.

What You Need:
- Your new fossil mold

- Petroleum jelly

- Silly Putty modeling clay

What to Do:
1. Coat the plaster of Paris impression with petroleum jelly.
2. Push a piece of Silly Putty into the mold, pressing firmly so that it fills the whole mold, and then remove it.

What Happens and Why:
One side of the Silly Putty is now a statuelike cast of the mold. This is what happens when minerals seep into the fossil mold and harden. The minerals form a hard cast of the original organism.

Geological Time Chart

The history of life on Earth is divided into eons and eras, which are broken down into periods. In the Cenozoic era, the periods are further broken down into epochs.

Era or eon	Years ago	Period	Epoch	Description
Archan eon	4.6 billion–1.5 billion			Earth formed; one-celled organisms
Proterozoic eon	1.5 billion–600 million			Primitive organisms, including bacteria and algae
Paleozoic era	600 million–500 million	Cambrian		Marine invertebrates (no backbones)
	500 million–440 million	Ordovician		Algae and seaweeds
	440 million–400 million	Silurian		Air-breathing animals
	400 million–350 million	Devonian		Fishes; amphibians; ammonites
	350 million–270 million	Carboniferous		More land areas; insects; reptiles
	270 million–220 million	Permian		Many reptiles

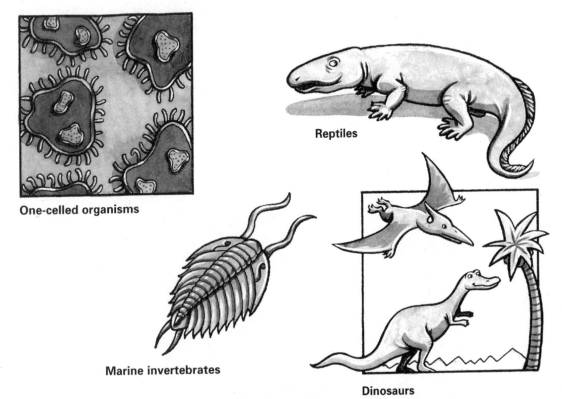

One-celled organisms

Reptiles

Marine invertebrates

Dinosaurs

Geological Time Chart (continued)

Era or eon	Years ago	Period	Epoch	Description
Mesozoic era	220 million–180 million	Triassic		Volcanic activity; marine reptiles; dinosaurs
	180 million–135 million	Jurassic		Dinosaurs
	135 million–65 million	Cretaceous		Extinction of dinosaurs and giant reptiles
Cenozoic era	65 million–60 million	Tertiary	Paleocene	Birds; mammals
	60 million–40 million		Eocene	Modern mammals
	40 million–25 million		Oligocene	Saber-toothed cats
	25 million–10 million		Miocene	Grazing mammals
	10 million–1 million		Pliocene	Prehistoric human ancestors; cooling climate
	1 million–10,000	Quaternary	Pleistocene	Development of humans; glaciers
	10,000–present		Holocene	Development of humans

Birds

Saber-toothed cats

Grazing mammals

Humans

Changing Fossils

Scientists who studied the fossils from different periods in Earth's history were puzzled about the changes that took place in similar organisms over time. A type of shellfish found in an old layer of rock, for example, may show up again in a younger layer of rock, but with a slightly different appearance, such as a **smaller** size. Studying different generations of fossils showed that the structure of plants and animals obviously changed over time. The big question in the scientific world was—*why?*

The answer came in the work of two scientists, Alfred Russel Wallace (1823–1913) and Charles Darwin (1809–1882). Working at the same time but not together, they each developed the theory of **natural selection.** Darwin's famous book *Origin of Species: A Theory of Natural Selection* was published in 1859. This book explains why nature provides plants and animals in such great variety. Some will be better than others at surviving. Those that survive will pass on some of their characteristics to the next generation. The unique characteristics of survivors stay on, while the unique characteristics of nonsurvivors fade away. Gradually, through each generation, the appearance of a plant or animal may change, or evolve. Natural selection provides an explanation for the gradual change, or **evolution,** of organisms. Evolution seems to be a positive development of living things. Each new generation is better able to survive than the previous one.

Dinosaur Rush!
Dino Bone
Digs

Dinosaurs may be extinct, but they're big stars in the modern world. Museums display whole dinosaur skeletons, glossy picture books portray what the dinosaur world may have looked like, and two of the most amazing special-effects movies of all time—*Jurassic Park* and *The Lost World*—breathe life into the mysterious, extinct reptiles.

Mary Anning: "The World's Greatest Fossilist"

A resort area called Lyme Regis along the southwest coast of England has been famous for hundreds of years for its limestone cliffs, which contain many fossils. In the late 1700s and early 1800s, tourists went to Lyme Regis to take in the fresh air and relax on the beach—and all of those who visited Lyme Regis wanted to take home a fossil.

Mary Anning was the popular owner of the most unusual shop on the beach. Her shop sold *only* fossils, primarily a variety of *ammonites*, extinct sea animals with a coiled outer shell. Mary Anning read everything she could find about fossils and organized her collection with great care. One of her most important discoveries was the first fossil of *Ichthyosaurus*, a fishlike reptile that lived in the sea more than 175 million years ago. Mary found this specimen when she was 10 years old! She is most famous for uncovering the first specimen of *Plesiosaur*, a long-necked sea reptile with flippers that swam in the sea from about 135 million to 200 million years ago.

Mary's reputation spread throughout Europe, and she became known as "the world's greatest fossilist." Her remarkable knowledge came from a lifetime of experience, disciplined study (all on her own), and a real talent for spotting fossils.

Before the 1800s, dinosaurs were total unknowns. No one knew that they had ever existed. Fossil hunters may have picked up a dinosaur tooth or bone, but no one had any idea what it was. Thanks to the work of geologists such as William Smith and Sir Charles Lyell, many people became fascinated with fossils, and fossil collecting became the hot new trend. The mid-1800s are known as the golden age of fossil collecting in England.

One of the most famous fossil collectors of the mid-1800s was Gideon Mantell (1790–1852), a physician. One day, when Dr. Mantell was making a house call, his wife tagged along. While she was waiting, she wandered around the patient's

estate, where she found a huge tooth partly buried in a rock. She uncovered it and gave it to her husband.

Dr. Mantell compared the tooth to those of living **reptiles**—cold-blooded animals that crawl or that walk on short legs, including snakes, turtles, and lizards. As a result, he learned that this tooth resembled the tooth of a South American lizard called an iguana. From this evidence, he suggested that the giant tooth came from a bigger, extinct version of the iguana, which he named *Iguanodon* (iguana tooth). Mantell wrote a book filled with fantastic illustrations of what some large extinct reptiles may have looked like, including the *Iguanodon*. His book, *Wonders of Geology*, was a smash best-seller, and dinosaur mania began!

Many bones from several kinds of large, extinct reptiles were discovered in the mid-1800s. In 1841, English scientist Sir Richard Owen announced his theory that these animals were not relatives of any living animals, but in a class by themselves. In a two-hour speech before a captivated audience, Owen called the extinct group *Dinosauria*. The animals in this group soon came to be known as dinosaurs. Owen took the name from the Greek words *deinos*, "monstrous," and *sauros*, "lizard."

Across the Atlantic, dinosaur-bone hunting took off in wild style! In the late 1870s, large deposits of dinosaur bones were uncovered in Colorado and Wyoming. These scientific treasures sparked the First Great Dinosaur Rush.

Fossil Bones in the White House!

Thomas Jefferson, the president of the United States from 1801 to 1809, was wild about fossils. Mammoth bones and other fossils in his growing collection were piled up on the floor of one of the rooms in the White House. Most of these fossils came from the western frontier, collected by explorers such as Lewis and Clark.

Dino Dining!

Several huge cement models of Dr. Gideon Mantell's creatures were created for the World Exhibition of 1851, a world's fair in London. A dinner party for a group of important scientists was held inside the hollow model of the *Iguanodon*!

The Second Great Dinosaur Rush took place in Alberta, Canada, around 1910. These discoveries provided many clues to what Earth was like during the late Cretaceous period, when dinosaurs roamed the entire planet.

In the early 1900s, major sites of dinosaur bones were uncovered in North America, Europe, Africa, and Asia. In 1922, a major exhibition set out for the Gobi Desert in Mongolia, the country that lies between Russia and China. This was fossil hunting on a grand scale—a small army of trucks and camels carrying scientists of many specialties. The scientists endured dust storms, scuffles with bandits, and equipment breakdowns, but the challenges were all worthwhile: The Gobi Expedition was the first to discover fossilized nests of dinosaur eggs among many dinosaur bones of the Cretaceous period.

Soon afterward, Mongolia was closed off from Western scientists for political reasons. Fossil exploration was not possible again until the doors of the country reopened in 1990. Since then, major expeditions have been very active in the Gobi Desert, digging up exciting new finds. In 1995, an expedition uncovered the first known nesting dinosaur, an ostrich-like creature called *Oviraptor*. Believed to have been killed in a sandstorm 80 million years ago, the *Oviraptor* died with its arms wrapped around at least 20 eggs tucked beneath its body. Scientists nicknamed this dinosaur Big Mama. This discovery revealed for the first time that dinosaurs acted with parental care.

Dinosaur fossils are found on every continent, including Antarctica. Rocks deposited as soft sediments between 65 and 220 million years ago may contain dinosaur fossils. These sedimentary rocks are common in the western United

The Dinosaur Feuds

Two nineteenth-century American paleontologists—Edward Drinker Cope and Othniel Marsh—started out as friends, but the First Great Dinosaur Rush out West made them bitter rivals in a race to dig up the most dinosaur bones. Their fighting became known as the Dinosaur Feuds. Cope and Marsh hired gun-toting fieldworkers and spies, and they tried to steal each other's shipments. Their legendary collecting efforts introduced the world to the most fascinating dinosaurs of all, including the grand *sauropods* (the giant, long-necked, plant-eating dinosaurs that walked on four legs).

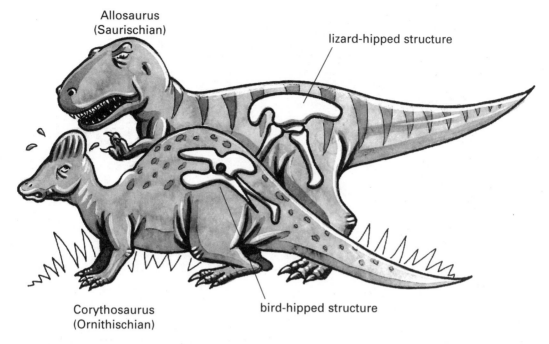

Allosaurus
(Saurischian)

lizard-hipped structure

Corythosaurus
(Ornithischian)

bird-hipped structure

Fossils of dinosaur skeletons reveal that dinosaurs are divided into two major groups, ornithischians and saurischians. Ornithischians, such as Corythosaurus, *often walked on four feet. Saurischians, such as the* Allosaurus *(the bigger, older relative of* Tyrannosaurus Rex*), usually walked on two feet.*

States and Canada. Dinosaurs lived in the eastern United States, too, but most of the sedimentary rock there was formed either before or after their existence. The only dinosaur fossils (mostly footprints) in that part of the country are from about 245 to 200 million years ago.

Dinosaur Fossils: Windows to a Lost World

T
he Mesozoic era, from 65 million to 220 million years ago, is known as the Age of the Dinosaurs. Fossils discovered throughout the world reveal that dinosaurs came in many different sizes and shapes. Fossilized dinosaur teeth reveal which ones were *carnivores* (meat eaters) and which were *herbivores* (plant eaters).

The study of dinosaur skeletons showed that all dinosaurs fall into two major groups, based on the type of hip bones they have. The hip structure of an *ornithischian* ("bird-hipped") dinosaur is similar to the hip structure of birds. Many ornithischians walked primarily on four legs, and sometimes on two. The second

Stegosaurus

type, *saurischian* ("lizard-hipped"), had a hip structure like that of modern-day lizards, and most of them walked on two legs.

Ornithischians were plant eaters, and some of the most common were the **hadrosaurs,** duck-billed dinosaurs. During the Cretaceous period, there were more duckbills than any other type of dinosaur. Duckbills, such as the *Corythosaurus*, had a flat beak at the front of the mouth and hundreds of teeth in the back of the mouth. Standing on four legs, they grew up to 9 feet (2.7 m) tall and over 30 feet (9 m) long. Another famous ornithischian was the North American dinosaur *Stegosaurus*, identified by the huge, upright bony plate running along its back.

Saurischians were the largest and fiercest of the dinosaurs. Well-known saurischians include the giraffelike *Brachiosaurus*, with a long neck that gave it a height of 40 feet (12 m) or more. *Tyrannosaurus rex* ("tyrant-lizard king") was the most feared meat-eating monster of its time. It would eat any dinosaur it could catch in its huge jaws filled with teeth 6 inches (15 cm) long. This dinosaur lived in western North America and western Mongolia.

Building a Dinosaur

Rarely is a complete dinosaur skeleton found. Weathering and the pressure of being buried in rock for millions of years destroys most of the bones. How do paleontologists construct an accurate model of a

Tyrannosaurus rex

dinosaur body from just a few bones? One of the biggest clues to how a dinosaur body looked is found in marks on the bones called **muscle scars.** These marks form where muscles attached to the bones, and the larger the scar, the bigger the muscle. Muscle scars reveal the size of the dinosaur, how the limbs attached to the rest of the skeleton, how the dinosaur held its head, and other aspects of the body.

Although rare, some fossils contain thin impressions of dinosaur skin. These impressions show whether the skin was scaly or smooth. The color of dinosaur skin does not survive, however, and paleontologists have to make a guess at what it may have been. The best guess is that dinosaur skin was similar to the color of their modern relatives—reptiles and birds.

Biggest and Smallest Dinosaurs

The biggest dinosaur was the *Seismosaurus*, which was longer than three school buses (about 138 feet [42 m]) and weighed more than nine elephants (35 tons [32 metric tons]). The *Seismosaurus* was recently discovered in New Mexico.

The smallest known dinosaur was the *Compsognathus*, which was about the size of a chicken.

What's in a Name?

Dinosaur names are made up of combinations of Greek or Latin words. The name often describes the dinosaur's appearance, but it also can describe where the fossil was found or the person who discovered it. Here is a list of Greek and Latin root words used to name dinosaurs.

Root word	Meaning	Root word	Meaning
anato	duck	mega	large
ankylo	crooked	micro	small
anuro	no tail	mono	one
archi	primitive	ops	face
brachio	arm	pachy	thick
bronto	thunder	ped	foot
cephalo	head	plateo	flat
cerat, ceros	horn	proto	first
compso	pretty	raptor	plunderer
cory, corytho	helmet	rex	king
di	two	saur, sauro, saurus	lizard
dino	terrible	stego	roof
diplo	double	tri	three
docus	beam	tyranno	tyrant
don, dont	tooth	urus, uro	tail
gnathus	jaw	veloci	speedy

Use the table to translate the following dinosaur names:

Anatosaurus   _____

Ankylosaurus   _____

Brachiosaurus   _____

Compsognathus   _____

Corythosaurus   _____

Diplodocus   _____

Pachycephalosaurus   _____

Plateosaurus   _____

Stegosaurus   _____

Triceratops   _____

Velociraptor   _____

Make up your own imaginary dinosaur by combining root words. How about a thick-faced, two-headed dinosaur, the *Pachyopsdicephalosaurus!* (Okay, I promised no more huge words like uniformitarianism. You can get back at me by making up an even longer word!)

New Dinosaurs!

Paleontologists are searching for dinosaur bones on every continent on Earth. With all this digging, a new kind of dinosaur is discovered *every six weeks!*

Human Fossils

About 5,500 years ago, people invented writing and began to record the history of their lives. Before that time, the only clues left behind about human life are found in fossils and ancient tools. The period of human life before the invention of writing is called **prehistory,** and human beings who lived in prehistory are called **prehistoric people.** From the fossil frenzies of the 1800s to the current day, scientists have made discoveries of many prehistoric human fossils. Fossils give clues to what prehistoric people looked like, how long they lived, what they ate, and what kinds of social groups they lived in.

Fossils show a long, gradual evolution of human beings that spans about the past 4 million years. From 2 million to 4 million years ago, the earliest human-like creatures lived throughout the southern half of eastern Africa. One of the most famous fossils in the world, Lucy, is a nearly complete skeleton of one of these prehistoric human ancestors. Lucy was found in Ethiopia in 1974. Lucy's group of ancient ancestors is called *Australopithecus* ("southern ape").

The next group of prehistoric people was *Homo habilis*, which means "handy human." These individuals were the first to use stone tools. Fossils of prehistoric people who lived from about 400,000 to 2 million years ago make up the group *Homo erectus* ("upright human"). *Homo erectus* people lived very differently than did their ancestors. Fossilized skulls of *Homo erectus* are bigger than those of *Australopithecus* and *Homo habilis*, and bigger skulls can hold larger, more intelligent brains. *Homo erectus* people were strong and muscular men and women. The tools found near *Homo erectus* fossils reveal that they were the first prehistoric people known to use fire and to hunt.

About 300,000 to 400,000 years ago, *Homo erectus* evolved into *Homo sapiens* ("wise human"). Fossil bones of *Homo sapiens* found in Africa, as well as Germany, China, France, and Israel, lead scientists to believe that these were the first prehistoric people to venture out of Africa.

Nariokotome Boy

One of the major human fossil discoveries of all time was made in Africa in 1984. Near the western edge of Lake Turkana, Kenya, scientists uncovered almost the entire skeleton of a *Homo erectus* boy. This thrilled scientists because until then, *Homo erectus* fossils only consisted of parts of the skull and a few other pieces of bone or teeth. The boy, about 11 or 12 years old, was tall for his age when he died—about 5 feet 8 inches (173 cm). The fossil skeleton, called Nariokotome boy, was found in rock near the Nariokotome River, which is usually a dry riverbed.

Neanderthals were a type of *Homo sapiens* who lived in Europe and the Middle East from about 130,000 to 35,000 years ago. They are named for the Neander Valley in Germany, where the first *Neanderthal* fossil was found in 1856. The most complete fossil skeleton of a *Neanderthal*, called "Old Man" of La Chapelle-aux-Saints, was **found** in France in 1908. With the discovery of carefully buried skeletons of men, women, and children, scientists learned that *Neanderthals* were the first human beings known to bury their dead.

When Is a Tooth Like a Tree?

The main fossils that identify prehistoric people are teeth. Hard teeth survive better than any other part of the body. Scientists measure the age of the person at death by counting lines on the teeth. Under a microscope, the outer surface of an *incisor tooth* (one of the four front teeth, top and bottom) contains very tiny ridges or ripples. The line that separates one ripple from another represents about seven days of growth. Count the lines, and you've got the age of the tooth. This is similar to counting tree rings, the lines found in the cross-section of a tree trunk. Each tree ring represents one year of growth.

Tracks of Wonder

The oldest known footprints made by *Homo sapiens* were recently discovered at Langabon, South Africa. A pair of footprints, each $8\frac{1}{2}$ inches (22 cm) long, have been preserved in rock for 117,000 years. The ripple-shaped rock is a sand dune that had hardened into rock. Geologist David Roberts found the footprints by accident one day in 1996. He was getting a little bored at a picnic, so he started running up and down some rock slopes. He spotted some chipped rocks and looked closer to discover that they were actually old stone tools. Some fossilized hyena prints were also nearby. Roberts decided that there was a one-in-a-million chance of finding human footprints, too, so he kept looking. A few hours later, he found them!

Why are footprints so rare? A very special combination of events has to take place to preserve them. The prints have to be made on the right type of ground. The rock has to harden around the footprints before the desert wind brushes them away. Thousands of years later, the rock has to break apart in just the right way to expose the prints. Finally, the prints must be discovered before weathering erases them. It's a one-in-a-million shot!

Including the Langabon prints, only four sets of early human footprints have been discovered. Two sets from Africa are of *Australopithecus*. A set found in England, which hasn't been dated yet, is thought to have been left more recently than the Langabon prints.

The next evolution of *Homo sapiens* was discovered in fossils about 100,000 years old. Named *Homo sapiens sapiens* ("wise, wise human"), these were the first modern people, like you and me. As compared with those of *Homo sapiens*, the skulls of *Homo sapiens sapiens* are higher and more rounded, the faces are smaller, the forehead is higher, and the large browridge above the eyes is gone.

How to Be a
Rock Hound

COLLECTING ROCKS,
MINERALS, AND FOSSILS

I hope this book has sparked your interest and curiosity in the treasures that lie in (and on) Earth's crust. The most satisfying way to learn more about rocks, minerals, and fossils is to collect them yourself. Where do you start?

The best place to look for rocks is in an **outcrop,** an area where the bedrock is exposed. **Bedrock** is the solid

Rock Hound Ground Rules

- Don't trespass! Always get permission from the *landowner* (a person or a company) before looking for samples.

- Bring an adult! Never take a rock-hunting trip without adult supervision.

- Do not litter or otherwise disturb the natural environment.

rock beneath the soil level. Outcrops can be found along the banks of rivers or streams, on beaches, in cliffs and quarries, and alongside roads and railroads that have been cut through rock. Another place to find rocks, especially granite, marble, and limestone, is at a stone-cutting factory that makes monuments, tabletops, or other stone objects.

To find out more, visit or call the rock shop nearest you, and ask whether there are any rock-collecting groups in your area. This is a great way to team up with other rock hounds on organized excursions. Buy a full-color field guide to rocks and minerals, and look up the facts about rocks in your region at a local library.

The geologic department of your state government has detailed maps of the types of rocks in many parts of the state. Ask your librarian to help you find the address of the office, and write to the people there, requesting a **geologic map** of the area in which you would like to look for rocks or fossils. The map contains coded information about the type of rock to be found. If your state cannot provide you with a map, request one from the United States Geological Survey (see the address in the Appendix).

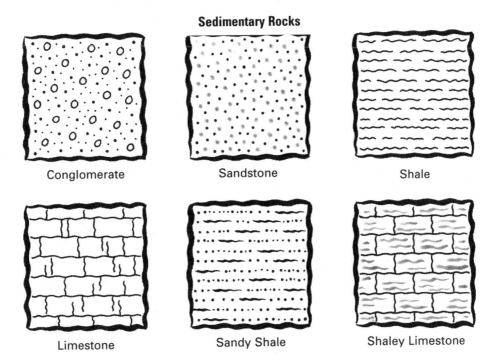

Sedimentary Rocks

Conglomerate

Sandstone

Shale

Limestone

Sandy Shale

Shaley Limestone

Igneous and Metamorphic Rocks

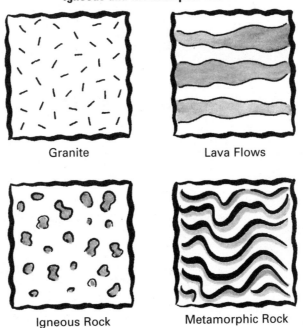

Granite

Lava Flows

Igneous Rock

Metamorphic Rock

In a natural setting, rocks loosely lying about are called **float.** These rocks may not represent the bedrock of the area. Float may have been carried from other locations more than 10,000 years ago by glaciers. If you collect float, it may be difficult to identify from geologic maps of the local area.

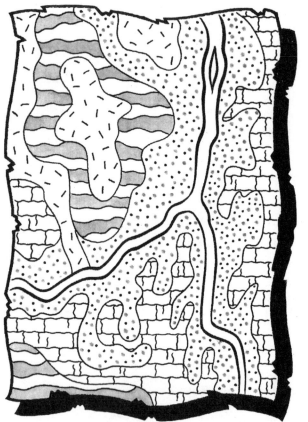

With the help of a geologic map, you can set out to find specific types of rock.

Peparing Your Collection

Basic rock-collecting tools include the following:

- Goggles, to protect your eyes from flying bits of rock
- Protective gloves
- Geologist's hammer, for removing rock samples (This type of hammer includes a chisel head for splitting rock.)
- Chisel
- Club hammer (sledgehammer) to use with a chisel (The thin chisel edge is placed in a rock crack and pounded in with the hammer to break apart the rock.)
- Trowel, for digging in clay
- Canteen or other water-filled container
- Sieve, for sorting rocks or fossils out of clay (Pour water over the clay in the sieve, to separate the specimens from the soil.)
- Small paintbrushes, for uncovering fossils

- Geologist's metal spatula, for cutting around fossils
- Tweezers and dental pick, for fine fossil work at home
- Magnifying glass
- Newspaper or sealable plastic bags, for wrapping specimens
- Clean, empty pill bottles or plastic tubes, for packing small specimens
- Light-colored masking tape to place on the newspaper or bottles (Write down a quick identification of the location or type of rock on the tape.)
- Notebook and pencil
- Camera, to make a permanent record of specimens
- Shoe box in which to carry specimens home
- Field guide to rocks and minerals, for accurate identification

In your collecting notebook, identify one page for each specimen. Include the date, the location, and a description of the rock. How **big** are the grains? What is the color or the mix of colors? What type of rock is supposed to be found in this location, according to your geologic map? If you have a camera, take a picture of each specimen **where** you found it. This will remind you of the rock formation that each piece in your collection came from.

Geologist's tools

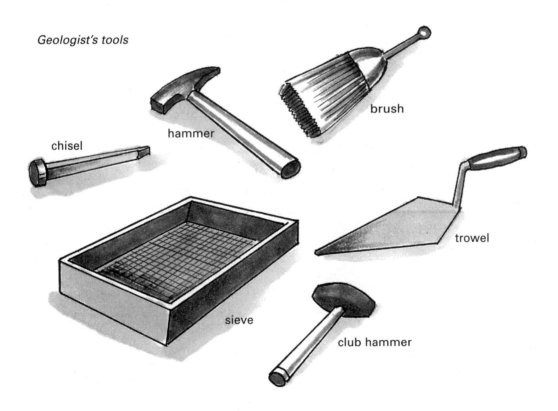

chisel

hammer

brush

sieve

trowel

club hammer

July 5, 1998
Connecticut River Bank,
Essex

Possible Limestone
light colored

When you get home, wash each rock sample thoroughly. Check your field guide, to make an exact identification of each rock.

Fossils can be found in any type of sedimentary rock, from shale and sandstone to limestone and conglomerates. Use the geologic maps to find sedimentary rock areas. Once you find a fossil embedded in the rock, carefully use the hammer and chisel to cut that portion of rock from the formation. When you get the sample home, use a smaller chisel, tweezers, and a dental pick to chip away at the rock that surrounds the fossil. Don't be in a hurry! Uncovering a fossil takes time and patience. Paleontologists work for many years to prepare fossils that go on display in museums.

If you want to learn more about your fossil find, take it to the paleontology department of a local university, or to a natural history museum. You may have found something important!

Displaying Your Collection

D isplay your rocks and fossils, complete with their labels, in small jewelry gift boxes or in shoe boxes with paper dividers. Create an index card for each specimen. In one upper corner, write the initial for the basic rock family: "I" for igneous, "S" for sedimentary, "M" for metamorphic, or "F" for fossil. Also include on the index card information from your collector's notebook, such as the date and location of your find. Arrange your collection in the four main groups. Paper-clip the photograph of the sample to the back of the index card.

Rock samples can also be transformed into smooth, shiny, personal gems with a rock polisher. Save up your allowance, or ask for one for your next birthday. You can make jewelry out of your polished rocks for yourself or as homemade gifts. You can go to a hobby or rock shop to buy the metal parts of the jewelry, such as the chains for a necklace or a bracelet or rings. Most rock polishers come with instructions about which type of glue to use to attach the polished stones to jewelry settings. Jewelry that you make yourself is a one-of-a-kind treasure.

July 5, 1998   S
Sandstone
River Bank of Connecticut River, beneath
the county Road 2 bridge near Essex

Appendix

ROCKY RESOURCES

Following are addresses of the offices of a few geological organizations in the United States. You can write to these offices and request information on rock and fossil sites that are open to the public.

United States Geological Survey
General Services Building
18th and F Streets, NW
Washington, DC 20242

Colorado Geological Survey
1313 Sherman Street, Room 715
Denver, CO 80203

State of Connecticut
Department of Environmental
  Protection
State Office Building
Hartford, CT 06115

(One brochure to ask for is
Fossils of the Connecticut Valley
by Edwin H. Colbert.)

Montana Bureau of Mines and
  Geology
Publications Office
Montana Tech, Main Hall
Butte, MT 59701

New Mexico Bureau of Mines
  and Mineral Resources
Socorro, NM 87801

Utah Geological and Mineral Survey
606 Black Hawk Way
Salt Lake City, UT 84108

Geological Survey of Wyoming
P.O. Box 3008, University Station
Laramie, WY 82071

(Ask for *Fossils of Wyoming* by Michael W.
Hager and *Traveler's Guide to Geology of Wyoming,*
in addition to any other brochures they have
available.)

Glossary

absolute time: a description of the age of rocks and fossils in terms of actual years.

amber: the sap of ancient trees, which has hardened into a solid.

asteroid: a solid, rocklike object found in the solar system, considered a small planet.

asteroid belt: a group of more than 100,000 asteroids, which revolves around the sun in the large space between the orbits of Mars and Jupiter.

atmosphere: the layer of gases surrounding Earth.

aureole: a region of rock that has been altered by the heat of nearby magma.

batholith: a large rock formation beneath Earth's surface, formed when a pool of magma cools over thousands of years.

bedrock: the solid rock beneath the soil level.

cabochon: a style of gem-cutting in which the stone is formed and polished into a smooth, rounded shape.

chemical sediment: sedimentary rock formed from minerals that were once held in water; when the water evaporates, the minerals harden into rock.

clastic sediments: sedimentary rocks made of rock particles ranging in size from fine particles of clay to boulders.

cleavage: a smooth, flat break formed when a mineral breaks along planes that reveal the mineral's crystal structure.

comet: an object made of dust, water, chemicals, and gas that orbits around the sun.

complex crater: a bowl-shaped dent in Earth's surface, with a hill-shaped structure rising from the floor, formed from a very powerful meteorite impact.

compound: a substance made of two or more elements, such as water (made from hydrogen and oxygen).

convection current: the movement of hot liquid or air to a cooler region.

coprolite: animal excrement preserved in fossilized form.

crystal: a solid, natural object with a structure formed of a repeating pattern.

dyke: a rock formation that rises up through layers of rock in a wall-like structure.

element: a chemical substance that cannot be broken down into a smaller unit (except the atoms that form it); elements are the basic structures of all objects on Earth, both organic and nonorganic.

emerald: a green gemstone formed from the mineral beryl.

erosion: the process by which wind and rain break down rock.

evolution: the gradual change of organisms over a long period of time, through the process of natural selection.

extinct: the description of a living organism that has died out as a species.

extrusive igneous rock: rock formed when lava erupts from volcanoes and cracks in the Earth, flows to the surface, and hardens.

faceted cut: a style of gem-cutting in which the stone is shaped into a pattern of highly polished, flat planes that act as mirrors.

fireball: a meteor that burns very brightly as it falls to Earth.

float: rocks that lie loosely on Earth's surface.

fossil: the remains or traces of a living thing.

fossil mold: an indented region found in rock, which is the exact shape of a leaf, shell, bone, or other fossil.

friction: the force that causes heat when two objects rub against each other.

fusion crust: the dark, thin outer layer of a meteorite, caused when friction melted the rock as it burned through Earth's atmosphere.

gemstone: a rare, hard mineral formed deep in the Earth, prized for its color and shape.

geode: a hollow rock containing crystals that form on the rock's inside wall.

geologic map: a coded guide to the types of rocks in a region.

geology: the study of the physical structure of Earth.

gold leaf: gold that has been pounded into an extremely thin sheet.

grains: mineral particles in rocks; large grains can be seen unaided, and smaller grains can be seen only with a microscope.

hadrosaur: a duck-billed dinosaur; the most common type of dinosaur during the Cretaceous period.

igneous rock: rock formed from magma inside Earth, which cools and hardens.

imprint: the fossil mold of a thin object such as a leaf.

intrusive igneous rock: rock formed below the surface of Earth when magma squeezes up into a cooler level of the crust and hardens.

iron: a meteorite made primarily of the elements iron and nickel, originally the central core of an asteroid; also a mineral element.

laccolith: a rock formation in the shape of a dome that pushes up the crust above it.

lava: molten rock that has escaped to the surface of Earth through volcanic activity.

lithification: the natural process of forming stone.

luster: the quality of a mineral's reflected light.

magma: melted rock material found in the mantle layer of Earth.

malleability: the quality of a metal that allows it to be pressed into various shapes without breaking.

mantle: the layer of molten rock that lies beneath Earth's crust.

mare basalt: a moon rock formed on the dark, smooth landscape of the moon.

metal: a hard, shiny solid formed when liquid and gas rise out of magma beneath Earth's surface.

metallic: having a shiny and sparkling quality, used to describe the luster of some minerals, such as gold.

metamorphic rock: igneous or sedimentary rock that has been changed into another type of rock through the forces of heat and pressure deep inside the Earth.

meteor: a rock from space, which enters Earth's atmosphere, burns, and forms a streak of light as it falls to Earth.

meteor shower: an event in which many meteors fall through Earth's atmosphere every hour.

meteorite: a meteor that has fallen to the surface of Earth.

midocean ridges: mountain ranges that wind along Earth's ocean floors.

mineral: a nonliving (inorganic), solid, natural substance.

mineralogist: a scientist who studies minerals.

muscle scar: the mark on a dinosaur bone formed by the muscle that was once attached to it.

natural selection: the process in nature in which the hardiest members of a species survive to the next generation.

nucleus: the solid, central part of a comet.

nutrients: nourishing substances found in soil, which are essential to plants and animals that eat them.

opal: a gemstone containing tiny bits of rainbow-colored silica within a solid body color.

opaque: the appearance of a mineral through which light cannot pass.

ore: a naturally formed solid containing a metal; the metal must be separated from the ore before it can be used.

organic sediment: sedimentary rock made from the remains of living things such as plants and shellfish.

outcrop: an area containing exposed bedrock.

paleontology: the study of extinct life forms.

petrified wood: the remains of ancient trees, which have filled with minerals and hardened into rock.

petrology: the study of rocks; a special division of geology.

plane: one of the flat surfaces that makes up a mineral's structure.

prehistoric people: human beings who lived during prehistory, beginning about 4 million years ago.

prehistory: the period before the invention of writing.

quartz rock crystal: a gemstone formed of clear, glasslike quartz.

radioactivity: the natural process by which certain elements change themselves into different elements, at a set rate of speed; radioactivity allows geologists to date rocks and fossils in absolute time.

regolith: the thin layer of small rocks covering the moon's surface.

relative time: a description of the age of rocks and fossils as existing before or after other rocks and fossils.

reptile: a cold-blooded animal that crawls or that walks on short legs, such as a snake, a turtle, or a lizard.

rock: a natural solid object made of one or more minerals.

rock cycle: the process in which rock is continually broken down and constructed through natural events, including erosion and rock formation.

ruby: Earth's rarest gemstone, formed from the red variety of the mineral corundum.

sapphire: a gemstone formed from the blue variety of the mineral corundum.

satellite: an object that moves in an orbit around a larger object.

seafloor spreading: the slow, constant movement of oceanic crust away from both sides of a midocean ridge.

sediment: particles of rock that are carried in streams and rivers to the seas, where they eventually sink to the ocean floor.

sedimentary rock: rock that forms in horizontal layers via the hardening of sediment.

shatter cones: cracks that form in the rock beneath a crater, due to the impact of a meteorite.

silicates: the most common family of minerals, made of the elements oxygen and silicon.

sill: a rock formation that spreads out between rock layers to create a horizontal sheet of igneous rock.

simple crater: a smooth, bowl-shaped dent in Earth's surface.

solar wind: a stream of particles of energy flowing from the sun.

solution: a liquid that contains dissolved substances.

stone: the most common type of meteorite, with a mineral makeup similar to Earth rocks; also another word for rock.

stony-iron: a meteorite containing a mixture of stone and iron, formed from the core–mantle layer of an asteroid.

streak test: a method of identifying a mineral by the color of the mineral when it's in powder form.

symmetry: in a crystal, the mirror positioning of flat surfaces that are opposite each other.

tectonic plates: the pieces of Earth's crust that carry the continents and move around on the mantle.

tektite: a glossy, smooth rock formed when small blobs of molten rock fly out from the impact site of a meteorite.

translucent: the appearance of a mineral through which some light can pass.

transparent: the appearance of a mineral through which light can pass completely, as in clear glass.

vein: a branchlike structure in which metals form in cracks of rock deep within Earth.

volcanic glass: a rocklike object formed when minerals harden very quickly into a solid mass without a crystal pattern.

weathering: the process by which chemicals and temperature changes weaken the structure of rock.

zap pit: a tiny hole appearing on the surface of a basalt moon rock, formed when a sand-grain-size meteorite struck the rock.

Index